Jackie Stewart

World Driving Champion

by Lyle Kenyon Engel
and the Editors of Auto Racing magazine

Jackie Stewart

World Driving Champion

ARCO PUBLISHING COMPANY, INC.
New York

Published by ARCO PUBLISHING COMPANY, INC.
219 Park Avenue South, New York, N.Y. 10003
Copyright © Lyle Kenyon Engel, 1970
All Rights Reserved
Library of Congress Catalog Number 76-117343
ISBN 0-668-02338-4
Printed in the United States of America
Typography by Elroy

Editorial Staff

George Engel
Marla Ray

Text

Elizabeth Hayward

Photography

David Phipps

Supplemental Photography

Eric della Faille
Beverly Engel
Joe Farkas
Ford Motor Company
Ford of England
Geoffrey Goddard

Indianapolis Motor Speedway
Bud Jones
Larry D. Kincaid
John May
John Plow
Nigel Snowdon

Contents

Introduction to
a Champion

Jackie Stewart, born John Young Stewart in Scotland on June 11, 1939, became the World Driving Champion on September 7, 1969 at Monza, in the Italian Grand Prix. He won the race by about half a car's length from Jochen Rindt, but he had already pulled out such a lead in the Championship, with five victories out of the seven Grands Prix thus far run, that he only had to finish the race to clinch the matter. But it is not Jackie's way to settle happily for anything less than first, and he won at Monza in a very convincing manner after a race-long slipstreaming extravaganza.

1969 was certainly *the* year for Stewart—as 1968 might well have been if

The 1969 World Champion in his Matra Ford MS80. Stewart led at one time or the other in all eleven of the GP races and won six of them.

9

The Stewarts have a magnificent view of Begnins from their garden.

he had not cracked a bone in his wrist when he had an accident in a Formula 2 car in Spain very early in the season. This caused him to miss the Spanish and the Monaco Grands Prix altogether, and when he returned to racing at Spa, in Belgium, he led the second half of the race—with his wrist still in plaster—only to run out of fuel on the last lap. This was a cruel disappointment, but he bounced right back to take the Dutch Grand Prix, leading from lap two till the fall of the checkered flag.

The "gnome of Begnins" relaxing on the grounds of his luxurious home in Switzerland.

11

Although his wrist injury was still giving him a lot of pain, he continued to drive brilliantly for the rest of the 1968 season. Sometimes after a race his arms would be swollen almost to the elbow, and his hand rubbed sore from the edge of the plastic support he then wore for driving, but it didn't prevent his winning the German and the American GPs by leading from start to finish. At the end of the season, in spite of the two missed races, he was still only three points behind Graham Hill and on an equal footing with Denny Hulme. He went to Mexico with every chance of overtaking Graham for the Championship. But Hill won, Hulme retired, and Jackie came in seventh, having dropped back from the lead with fuel pressure trouble.

It was a very near thing, and the final result was a great tribute to Stewart's tenacity. The narrowness of his defeat gave him an extra determination to win when the 1969 season began, and he was helped by having the most reliable car on the circuits at a time when it mattered most, and by the superb organization of the Tyrell/Matra team, with the invaluable cooperation of Dunlop. Stewart gives constant and unstinting credit to these major factors in his success, stressing time and again that it was very much a team effort. Ken Tyrrell, on the other hand, says their success was due to having "the best driver," and he is an honest and outspoken man, not given to false praise.

Jackie's Championship crown, then, was something for which he had worked very hard. Having achieved it, he works very hard at *being* the Champion, not merely for its commercial value, but out of loyalty to his sponsors and out of a passionate desire to have motor racing achieve the status and importance that he thinks it deserves. For this reason he has signed a contract with Mark McCormack, the American promoter who made golf a headline sport involving big money. Jackie has been much criticized for this in Europe, where it is still considered bad taste to talk about money, or to try to make as much of it as possible. His approach makes sense in the United States, where it is thought not only normal but praiseworthy, but in Europe he has had to contend with endless remarks beginning, "I know we have to pay to speak to you these days . . ." and he has been very patient with those who attack him, explaining his reasons for his connection with the McCormack organization.

"The biggest problem with motor racing today, particularly in Europe, is that until recently it has been a sport of amateurs. With ever-increasing costs,

The Stewart children: Mark (left) and Paul (right).

12

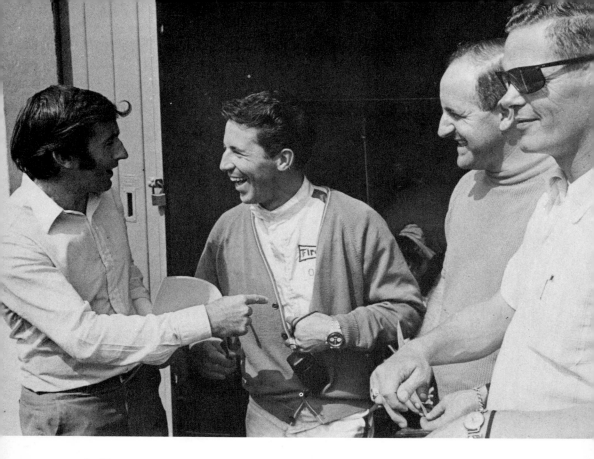

Jackie enjoys a good joke. Here he clowns with Mario Andretti prior to
practice for the 1968 Italian GP. Andretti and Bobby Unser (far right) were
not allowed to race, having participated in an event the day before. Stewart
dropped out with engine trouble and Denis Hulme (next to Unser) won.

something has got to be done to bring money into racing. I think it is most
important to popularize it, to bring it to the attention of a wider public. At
present it does not get anything like the attention it deserves, either in the
newspapers or on television, because it does not sell itself to the press. Even
in Britain, where it is one of the few sports in which the country is con-
sistently successful, it is not being properly reported. Motorcycling gets into
the sports pages but motor racing does not. Pigeon racing, bowls, even
croquet make the sports pages when motor racing does not—unless there has
been an accident. And yet it has far more color than a lot of other sports,
more drama and excitement, a tremendous collection of personalities—team
managers, car owners, mechanics and journalists as well as drivers. Motor
racing is very popular in Britain, and far more so in parts of Europe, and

14

America is getting keener every year—yet it is still the Cinderella of the sporting world."

Jackie is convinced that proper promotion and publicity could change all this, bringing in sponsors who have never before been involved. The fuel and tire companies have for many years poured money into motor racing without getting very much back, partly because they have not used their successes in the right way and have scarcely used their contracted drivers at all. Jackie has begun to change this pattern by working closely with Dunlop to publicize both their tires and his own achievements. He puts in a "plug" for them almost every time he speaks in public. He is appearing now in advertisements for articles not directly connected with racing and will do far more of this in the future.

Because he has become an astute businessman as well as a top racing driver, Jackie is often regarded as money-grubbing and too publicity-conscious, even by other drivers. His emigration to Switzerland brought the usual accusations about evading Income Tax, to the extent of alienating some of his fellow countrymen. Recently, a suggestion that Stewart should have a Champion's reception in his hometown was criticized because it was felt he had been disloyal to his country by evading its taxes. Jackie's reply was, "I don't want to drive for Harold Wilson half the year!" and anyone who is successful and making really good money in Great Britain today will echo his sentiments—the others have already left!

But there were other very good reasons for the Stewarts' move to Begnins, a small village in the Vaud region of Switzerland, about twenty miles from Geneva. They had previously lived in a large and very pleasant house in Dunbartonshire, with a view across the Clyde to the high moors of Ayrshire, and Jackie was commuting constantly.

"In 1965, 1966, and 1967 I was very busy, and it reached the stage where I was just going home to sleep. I was traveling between home, Glasgow and London airport winter and summer, sometimes in fog, sometimes in snow; sometimes I had to go by train. I was losing about a day a week just getting to races and back—and I couldn't keep it up. I was either going to lose my family, or stop motor racing. I was trying to run the family garage business when I *did* get home, and I was racing more than fifty times a year. I wasn't seeing Helen or my sons for more than a few hours a week.

"I had to decide—where was the best place to live? It had to be either London or the continent, and London would, in fact, have meant somewhere in Surrey where I could buy a house with enough land; the house in Scotland had an acre and a half, and I could see how the children were going to enjoy

it. And I decided that going to and fro between Surrey and London airport would be nearly as bad as commuting to Glasgow, so—Switzerland had two main advantages. Firstly, it is the center of Europe and therefore easy to get to from any direction, and it's a fabulous place to live in. The second reason was, quite frankly, financial."

The Begnins area appealed to them most, partly because it is near Geneva airport, partly because it is easier to establish residency in Vaud than in the city itself and partly because their old friends Joakim and Marianne Bonnier had lived nearby for several years and were at that time their only contacts in this foreign country. After living in a furnished flat for a while in the early summer of 1968, they bought the house which is now called "Clayton," as were the Stewarts' two previous homes in Scotland.

It is a beautiful house in a beautiful situation. All the main rooms face south, down over the farmland and the vineyards, across the Lake of Geneva to the spiky, white-topped Alps. The land surrounding Clayton House and owned by Jackie amounts to around six acres, most of it woodland. The gardens consist mostly of lawns and shrubs, and a broad terrace along the south side. The land drops away steeply from the house to the south and east, and rises quite steeply to the north, so that the house is sheltered from the worst weather.

Behind the heavy front door, with its big brass knocker, the atmosphere is warm and quiet and welcoming. It is easy to see why Jackie is always so anxious to get home. Comfort and relaxation have evidently been the Stewarts' main aims in decorating and furnishing their home, and once inside, one finds it difficult to summon up the energy and will power to leave. Possibly the main reason for this is Jackie's welcoming grin and twinkling eyes and his obvious pleasure in giving hospitality. Possibly Helen's quiet, unruffled acceptance of Jackie's many friends, and her unobtrusive efforts in the kitchen region also help to bring about this euphoria. My children disappear into the garden or into the playroom with the two Stewart children, Paul and Mark,

18

and then we tend to gravitate to Jackie's study and talk—and talk.

The study is a small, crowded room, with a wall lined with books, where Jackie has his desk and conducts his business deals over the telephone, or signs hundreds of pictures of himself to send out to fans. A sofa and a couple of armchairs and the sunshine pouring in from south and west make it a cosy intimate place, as opposed to the elegance of the enormous sitting room which has windows and doors opening out onto the terrace.

This room should really be called a "salon," for it has a decidedly French atmosphere. It leads directly off the hall, where a valuable marble table carries many of Jackie's silver cups and other awards—plus letters, invitation cards and any other literature that has recently been put through the front door!

At the southeast corner of the house is the dining room, with a vast oak table to seat twelve that Helen and Jackie brought from Scotland, with rush-seated, ladder-backed, country-style chairs and a dresser dating from about 1730. Behind this to the north is the kitchen, very modern, very clean, very efficient. The almost spiral staircase just outside in the passageway to the hall leads down to the basement. This is carefully fitted up as four separate units —laundry room, boiler room, a playroom for the children and a games room for Jackie, where he can play table tennis with his neighbor Jochen Rindt (and get beaten)!

Beyond Jackie's study is a guest suite, and up on the first floor there are four bedrooms; two for the boys, built on since their arrival and furnished with Nordic simplicity; the nannie's room and a large suite facing west for Jackie and Helen. This last is decorated mainly in pink and has a bed of almost Hollywood opulence and proportions which, apart from the hi-fi—hidden away in a seventeenth-century Scottish dower chest in the sitting room—is the Stewarts' only downright "show off" piece.

Astute with his money, careful as any Scot past or present, Jackie puts most of his expenditure into *comfortable* as opposed to ostentatious living. The household is run on a strict yearly budget. Helen has a dress allowance, and keeps within it. Jackie's flamboyant shirts and ties, which he has assumed over the past two years, are perhaps a natural contrast to the uniform of the racing driver. (There are several other snappy dressers on the party-time scene, including Graham Hill, Jo Bonnier, Jack Oliver, Jackie Ickx and Jochen Rindt.)

But Jackie Stewart is a lot more than a first-class racing driver and a business-minded Scot. He is a highly articulate exponent of the art of race driving, never at a loss for words during an interview either in private or on nationwide television. No one since Stirling Moss has been able to clarify the why and the how of the subject for the layman and for the cognoscenti quite so graphically. He is intensely aware of what he is doing, of its pleasures, its

dangers, its triumphs and its tragedies, and he can talk about them and bring them alive for other people. He lives at a pace and a pitch that some might describe as feverish, and the old cliché about climbing to the top of Mont Blanc but not being able to live there has been trotted out and gloomily used to imply that the amazing Stewart vitality must have its limits.

But Jackie is very much aware of his limits. He takes exactly as much rest as he needs, relaxing completely when he does get home to Switzerland, usually lying out on the terrace in the sun reading a book. Or he might play a round or two of golf. Or just romp with his two small sons. One, or maybe two days of this, and he's all ready to switch on to his other life again, testing tires, setting up his car, racing, appearing on television, talking to journalists, discussing technicalities, receiving awards, making speeches or going into a huddle with Ken Tyrrell and the Dunlop Rubber Company about the next race and future prospects.

Jackie is always ready to talk seriously about anything, though with a natural bias towards cars and racing. He has neither time nor patience for small talk. He likes a certain amount of gossip, as long as it is not malicious, and enjoys humorous anecdotes rather than jokes. If you would be his friend, or even if you just want to make a good impression, never "gush"; and if you don't know much about motor racing, don't talk to him about it at all. Tell him about yourself, your job, your successes; teach him something new. Don't start by telling him how marvelous you think he is. He will simply smile and make a polite reply and move away rapidly. He has excellent manners and a friendly disposition, but both have been stretched almost to the breaking point during the last few months by some of the more inane of the people who will always latch onto the current "lion."

Most Scots can detect a phony within seconds, and Stewart is no exception. What upsets him most of all is incompetence, "other people's shortcomings." "I get annoyed," he says, "by people who are highly paid to do a professional job, who are considered to be good, and then fail by not concentrating, not being professional. Or by not doing their homework. I'm not really bitchy with anybody, because I think if you are, it merely shows your own lack of professionalism. I should be able to take all kinds of people and rub them off my shoulders if they are doing the wrong thing. If I get myself upset it isn't doing *me* any good, let alone them."

His good humor and love of all kinds of music extends even to the pits and prompts him to try Chris Barber's trombone.

Common trackside sight around the world: Jackie Stewart in a huddle with Ken Tyrrell over lap times.

Helen says they have never had a row since they were married seven years ago, and I believe her. By keeping his good humor and philosophic view of life, even in the face of great disappointments and adversity, Jackie makes it virtually impossible for anyone to quarrel with him. He puts his case far too well, and the dominant factors in his character seem to be caution and sweet reason, allied to a strong ambition and an unusually clear idea of where he is going. He has reached the pinnacle of his profession in five crowded years. What goes towards the making of a Champion? In Jackie's case I think a large part of the answer can be found in his childhood in Scotland.

Background to Success

Dunbartonshire is a western county of Scotland, bordered by Loch Lomond, Loch Long and the Clyde estuary. The country around is hilly—mountainous in places—and Dumbarton is the county town, fifteen and a half miles from Glasgow. It is an old place, with a pedigree going back to known Celtic and Roman settlements, and it has both the dignity of its ancient origins plus the twentieth-century bustle and importance of an industrial town. About eight miles northwest along the estuary is Helensburgh, which was laid out in the eighteenth century as a "watering place" of some elegance. Both these towns and the countryside around them have played a large part in the life of Jackie Stewart.

He was born, lived and grew up in the village of Dumbuck, very close to Dumbarton. His father Robert, once a keen amateur motorcyclist, owned a garage business, and was a Jaguar and BMC agent. He had one other son, Jimmy, eight years older than Jackie. Bob Stewart's father was a gamekeeper, Head Gamekeeper in fact, for Lord Weir, a prominent Scottish industrialist who had a large estate at Eaglesham, in Renfrewshire.

"This had an influence on me," says Jackie, "because I was very fond of shooting from an early age. It was always an ambition to get a gun in my hand. This was not yet a competitive thing, it was just wanting to shoot."

The other great family sport was fishing, and most of the family holidays were spent by a stretch of the River Spey over which his father had fishing rights.

"I used to go up to the same stretch of river that I have now, in syndicate. I don't get there very often these days, but I love it when I can. My father

23

Young Jackie enjoyed fishing by a stretch of the river Spey over which his father had fishing rights.

has been going there for thirty-five years, and as children, my brother and I were taken to that place more than to any other.

"There was one holiday we had that was totally different. When I was about fourteen, I went with my mother to Canada and America. My father had been earlier. It was a big thing for me, I was very impressed. It came about because during the war my parents had run a taxi service as well as the garage, and their area included the Clyde docks. Tankers were coming in with oil for Britain, and we became friendly with some of the personnel, captains and so on, whom we used to drive around. I can remember doing these sort of trips, and of course they continued after the war as well. This trip to the States was in order to visit some of the good friends we made.

"I can remember it very clearly—New York, the Empire State Building, Niagara Falls, Canada. We went over on a stratocruiser, which was a big double-decked plane that took fourteen hours. I was very impressed by the whole thing."

Back home, the education of the younger Stewart boy was not going as well as it should. The standard of scholarship in Scotland is very high and lays a good deal of emphasis on the passing of examinations. Dumbarton Academy, which Jackie attended, has won a reputation for success in every academic field, but I don't think they had thought to produce a world class racing driver—it certainly wasn't in the curriculum.

Jackie says he neither liked nor disliked school. By the age of fourteen he was suffering from marked apathy.

"If the headmaster remembers me at all, it will be because I ought to have stayed on, that's all. I left at fifteen—I'd lost all interest. I think I was an average scholar, not brilliant nor particularly dumb. I didn't concentrate, that was my biggest failing. I never did concentrate on anything—though I enjoyed sports. I used to play football for the school, then the County. Yes, I was a bit competitive in school sports. As long as I can remember I've always wanted to have a go!"

25

Before he began racing he was very successful at clay pigeon shooting.

One reason for his lack of interest in the ordinary work of the Academy was his success in clay pigeon (or trap) shooting.

"I started shooting very early on, mostly rabbits, up behind our house. I was trained the right way. My father used to take me out to show me how to handle a gun and how to use it correctly. And he was a disciple of the etiquette of shooting. It had to be done exactly the right way.

"But, apart from the rabbits, there was nothing to shoot, so I started on clay pigeons. A clay pigeon trap is something anyone can buy, but in my case my grandfather had one. At the beginning of each season the Weirs or their guests would come up for a day's shooting to get their hand in before they started on the grouse. I just got a loan of the trap and went off and bought some clay pigeon targets and used to go up there every day after school. I could just about afford ten birds, or shots, at a time, and I was getting to the stage where I was hitting eight or nine or even ten out of ten. So I went in for a competition."

This was Jackie's first experience of having someone in direct competition with him—a challenging sensation. And he liked it. He won his first competition when he was fourteen.

"It was New Year's Day. I probably won because all the other Scotsmen were stoned! But that started the competition bug off—I wanted to enter every one there was."

This new enthusiasm, plus the fact that his brother Jimmy was now a racing driver and Jackie an ardent follower, did his school work no good at all, and he left the Academy to start work in the family garage.

"It was my father's business and I wanted to go into it. It was my ambition at that time to be a garage man. I had no hope and no great desire to do anything else. I started work on the forecourt, selling petrol, and I used to get £3.12.6 a week, plus about £3.15 in tips at the pumps. Then I went into the lubrication bay for a year, and that was when I started to serve my apprenticeship, because you have to be sixteen to do that. You serve a five-

year apprenticeship as a motor mechanic, or motor engineer. I went to night school and did all that bit. Then I went into the garage itself, as a mechanic, and by the time I was twenty or twenty-one I was looking after the tuning side of cars, specialist work which was coming into the garage by this time, mainly due to my brother's racing activities."

Meanwhile, Jackie's shooting was improving with every competition, and he became a superb marksman. His eye for distance, speed and trajectory, and his extraordinarily quick reflexes, which have come in so useful when aiming a racing car at the apex of a corner, took him to the top in shooting, too.

He was on the Scottish team in 1955, and in 1956 he won the West of England Championship. He was only seventeen.

"I remember it all very well, because it was my first trip out in my car. It was an Austin A35, spruce green, with Stewart tartan seat covers. An absolutely standard one, immaculate, polished twice a week. I drove down to Bournemouth to shoot, and won this thing, and drove back again, all on my own, which I enjoyed very much.

"My shooting played a big part in making me ready for the success that I have had in motor racing. It was of tremendous importance to me. Of course, it was an amateur business, and in fact cost me a lot of money; everything I had was put into it—I knew I wasn't going to get anything out of it financially, it was just a terrific pleasure. In fact, my pleasure at winning in shooting was a far more intense pleasure than I have ever experienced in motor racing. I'm sure I put more effort and dedication into it than I do now into racing. I have become a much more mellow person. Then I was so intense—too much so for success, really."

Intensity notwithstanding, Jackie went from strength to strength. By 1960 he was shooting so well he took the British, the Irish and the Scottish championships and won the Coupe des Nations, which is the European and Mediterranean championship.

His skill at clay pigeon shooting brought him many trophies. He won his first competition when he was fourteen and was Champion of the West of England when he was only seventeen. Four years later he won the British, the Irish and the Scottish Championships and won the Coupe de Nations, the European and Mediterranean Championships.

"The British and the Coupe des Nations I won in the same weekend, in North Wales. Of all the things that I have ever won, that gave me most pleasure, because I was much younger, much more impressed by success, and I won it fair and square against the best shots in the world."

After that came what he still regards as the greatest disappointment of his life, "worse than Indianapolis in 1966, worse than running out of fuel at Spa—or just missing the World Championship in 1968, for that matter."

He was in the last round of the trials for the Rome Olympics of 1960, and was leading. It was to be a two-man team, and it was practically a foregone conclusion that Jackie would be chosen. But he had the only off day he had experienced in two years, for no reason that he can imagine.

"I suddenly dropped eight targets out of twenty-five, and I found myself losing my place in the Olympics by one point. I was relegated to Reserve. It was my twenty-first birthday. I still feel annoyed about it—I didn't even get to travel to Rome at all. Here was something I *desperately* wanted to do, to be a member of the Olympic team. To be in the Olympics was something bigger than being a Formula One driver—it was *big*. And I was shooting very well that year."

Philosophical as he is, that one "off day" is something Jackie is never going to get over.

A. N. Other and Friends

Cars, together with the traditional Scottish pastimes of hunting, shooting and fishing, have been part of Jackie Stewart's life from as far back as he can remember. As a child he gravitated to the family garage as often as possible, poking his sharp nose, boy-like, into all available machinery. When he was about eleven his brother Jimmy was just starting in club racing, and Jackie immediately became a fan. He went with his brother to meetings whenever he could, taking along his autograph book and absorbing the essential atmosphere of motor racing.

Jimmy's career began with an MG/TC, and he soon graduated to a Healey Silverstone, in which his performances were impressive enough to engage the attention of the famous Scottish racing team, Ecurie Ecosse. He was asked to drive for them in 1953, and went on to get a factory drive with Aston Martin in 1954. It was at Le Mans that year that he suffered a very bad accident, and his parents, especially his mother, were not unnaturally turned against motor racing. The following year Jimmy tried to make a comeback at Silverstone in a D-type Jaguar, but in practice on his very first day he aquaplaned at Club Corner and turned the car over. About ten days later he went to the Nürburgring for the 1000ks, and turned the D-type over again, this time due to mechanical failure. But he was trapped underneath for about twenty minutes, and he decided to retire from the sport.

"All this time," Jackie says, "my mother was *very* anti-motor racing, and the subject became taboo in our house. She was very highly strung—still is—but in those days it affected her health badly, giving her skin problems and

Five-time World Driving Champion Juan Manuel Fangio was Jackie's greatest idol.

so on. I had never really thought of motor racing myself, although I enjoyed the sport as a youthful spectator. The drivers were my gods. Fangio, Ascari, and Moss—especially Fangio. Have a look at my autograph book."

He fetched a rather battered small brown book from his study shelves and showed me the hallowed names. A lot of them were very well known sports car drivers of the fifties, interspersed with a few of the Grand Prix stars gathered at Silverstone or Aintree. But among the famous motor racing signatures there were many from a very different scene, the world of music; mostly Scottish singers, but a few operatic stars.

"My father was a keen amateur," explained Jackie, "and we met quite a few of these people when they came to Glasgow. Music has always been of great importance to me. I enjoy a lot of things, from Bach and Beethoven to Frank Sinatra and the Beatles. Everyone knows I'm the Beatles Number One fan. But I've got a good selection of classical music as well, because, depending on my mood, they supply me with everything I want to hear."

Looking at the autograph book evidently brought back vivid memories of Jackie's early associations with motor racing, and prompted us to discuss exactly how he had made his own entry into the sport.

From 1955 onwards, while the subject was still taboo in the Stewart household, Jackie was concentrating hard on his clay-pigeon shooting, never satisified with less than first place, developing a keen eye, good coordination and a taste for success. Meanwhile, his apprenticeship as a motor mechanic progressed, and the garage became well-known in the west of Scotland for preparation and performance, mainly due to Jimmy's racing activities. For two or three years Jackie was spending his working hours tuning and preparing high performance cars, and he developed a taste for fast driving himself, moving on from the "spruce green A35" to a red Austin Healey.

It was at about this time that Barry Filer entered his life, a wealthy Scottish enthusiast who for family and business reasons couldn't continue racing himself, but who wanted to see his cars raced. Barry Filer was the catalyst which began the process of turning the young garage mechanic into a potential World Driving Champion.

Not that he marched along straight away with the offer of a drive for Jackie—far from it. He already had a driver, Jimmy McInnes. His two cars were a Porsche Super 90 and an AC Bristol.

"They were beautiful cars, immaculate in every way," recalls Jackie, "and I used to prepare them for Jimmy McInnes to drive. We used to do sprints and hill climbs and races, and I was his mechanic. The AC Bristol was the one he mainly raced. It was a gem to work on, like a new pin all the time.

34

This is Jackie's red Austin Healey which obviously impressed Helen.

I did all the usual things, warming it up, taking it to the line and all that sort of thing, and Jimmy used to drive it. He used to arrive on the grid with his crash helmet under his arm and just get in and drive the car. He's a very nice bloke, and it was part of my education to work with someone like that, in that capacity.

"Anyway, he did quite well, but he kept making the odd mistake—running over the odd five-gallon drum—and Barry suggested I might like to have a drive. I was scared stiff and refused, the first time he asked me. My mother had made it very clear that if I raced, either she left home or I left, and

He raced a Marcos at Charterhall and finished third his first time out.

anyway I was a bit apprehensive. I wasn't all that enthusiastic about motor racing at the time. So I refused Barry's offer."

However, the second time he was asked he accepted. By then he had had the chance to find out what it was like to drive a good car at speed on a circuit. Sometime during 1960, he and his good friend, motorcyclist Bob McIntyre, had gone down to Oulton Park, in Cheshire, primarily to find out whether Bob was going to be any good at motor racing.

"We went in the Bristol, with Barry's permission, and we both thrashed round there for a morning. It felt fabulous. A big, big thrill. I didn't know at the time how fast I'd gone, but I learned later that it was faster than the class record for these two liter cars. The sensation was so marvelous I couldn't imagine why we didn't do it all day, but Bob said he'd done an hour or so and had found out what he wanted to know—he'd decided to be a racing driver—and we ought to pack it in and go home. It was a heartbreak for me, I could have gone on all day."

That was really the beginning. Jackie had tasted the unique pleasure of driving fast on a circuit designed for racing, and "it felt fabulous." So when Barry Filer again suggested he race for him, Jackie accepted. Hiding under the pseudonym of A. N. Other, so that his mother should not discover what he was up to, he went in for a sprint at Heathfield, near Prestwick, in 1961 in the Porsche Super 90. He was second overall to a driver from Newcastle in a TVR, only a split second slower, but much faster than all the rest, which he describes as "pleasing."

Then Barry Filer built a Marcos, one of the first of the breed, with a 1000cc Ford engine. Jackie raced it at Charterhall, the Scottish circuit, and first time out he was third. In the second race he won his class. In all he raced at Charterhall four times in 1961, and in October we come across the first mention of J. Stewart, junior, in print in a national motoring magazine. *Autosport* relates, "Young Jackie Stewart hustled around in his blue Marcos, but, having a Ford engine, could not get to grips with the Climax-powered cars."

Later in the same report they say, of the Grand Touring Car race, "Jimmy Stewart was on the grid giving the benefit of his experience to young brother Jackie, driving an Aston Martin DB4, and *how* he benefited, as he ran away from Captain Ramsay's E-type coupe!" Jackie won that race. In the same results we see that Jim Clark took two second places in other events, driving what the reporter describes as "a somewhat worn Aston Martin DBR1." As Jimmy was already second driver to Innes Ireland in the Lotus Formula 1 team, and had long since served his club-racing apprenticeship, there is no reason to think that at that stage Clark would have singled Jackie out in any way from the other young Scots racing at Charterhall.

In 1962 Jackie again raced four times at the same circuit—and also got married. He had known Helen McGregor for five years. She came from nearby Helensburgh, where her mother kept a bakery, and Jackie had covered the road from Dumbuck many times in his red Austin Healey. Helen knew she was marrying a car enthusiast who went racing occasionally on weekends, but that, she thought, was all—just a hobby!

At the first meeting at Charterhall in April 1962, Jackie again drove the Marcos in the Sports Cars up to 1600cc race, and led from start to finish. The *Autosport* report continues, referring to the second race for GT cars, "In the up to 1300cc class, interest centered on the Thompson/Stewart dice, in which the latter's Marcos was neater through the swerves but was over-taken on the straights." He finished third.

Although he entered himself as A. N. Other until the following year, it is already obvious that the second of the Stewart boys was being noticed, and favorably. Jackie's father and brother knew what he was up to and encour-aged him—"My father let me have my head," as Jackie puts it. "It was a bit of a thrill for him. But we kept it from my mother."

Sitting on a Tojeiro with his brother Jimmy next to a D-Jaguar.

The newlyweds were living in a furnished flat, and Jackie was still very much the garage man working in the family business. By now they had an E-type Jaguar, which was the garage demonstrator, and Jackie kept his hand in by giving prospective customers either the thrill or the fright of their lives along the Dunbartonshire country roads.

The two brothers began to drift apart a bit after Jackie's marriage, but the crowd of new friends Jackie made inside racing were to last him till the present day. In 1963 they went everywhere in a troupe, all Scotsmen, and some are still racing. On Easter Saturday that year J. Y. Stewart went south of the border for the first time, to the airfield circuit of Rufforth, near York. It was a bleak, cold, wet day, and they took the E-type, "bog standard, except for a set of racing tires," and left at 4:45 in the morning.

The effort was worth it. Jackie entered two events, and won them both in pouring rain. It was a big meeting, organized by the British Racing and Sports Car Club, and for Jackie a big occasion. One report of the first event stated that it involved, ". . . a newcomer from Scotland in the shape of Jackie

Alberto Ascari, who was twice World Champion, was another of Jackie's idols.

Stewart with an E-type. Driving in the style of another of that name, he won just as he liked." Later on the writer says of the sixth event, "J. Stewart won with consummate ease."

The next month at Charterhall Jackie "burnt much rubber off the tires of a 3.4 Jaguar saloon" in the GTs over 1300cc, trying to catch up with an E-type belonging to a gentleman named Scarth. In a later race he took over Mr. Scarth's E-type and, "despite the wet track, Stewart romped off the line and shot through Lodge Corner into the lead"—which he never lost.

A pattern is already beginning to emerge, of a talented amateur collecting trophies from every meeting he enters, a driver who attracts attention, and in spite of racing only a few times a year, has enough natural ability to shine amongst the more experienced club drivers like a nugget of pure gold.

Recognition and Rewards

Ecurie Ecosse, never slow to spot native talent, attended a meeting at Ouston, near Newcastle, not long after Jackie's Rufforth outing. Scotland's most famous driver, Jimmy Clark, was running at Indianapolis for the first time (and, in fact, very nearly won) and was leading Grand Prix races from start to finish in the revolutionary Lotus 25. It was to be Clark's first World Championship year, with six GP wins and maximum points.

At Ouston, David Murray of Ecurie Ecosse was watching this other young Scotsman in an E-type Jaguar, who won his race against odds after calling at his pit to have a coil lead put back on. His smooth and determined driving impressed Murray, who had known him well since childhood through brother Jimmy, but did not automatically assume that young Jackie would be as good. However, the few races at Charterhall, plus his showing at Rufforth and Ouston, made up his mind for him. He asked Jackie to drive for the team for the rest of the '63 reason.

"This was a great moment for me," Jackie says, "I knew all the people

Ken Tyrrell gave Jackie his first single-seater ride in a Cooper T72 during a test session at Goodwood and was horrified at the speeds he was turning.

In 1964 he drove a Cortina Lotus to victory at Oulton Park in England and also at Marlboro in the United States.

concerned—David Murray, Wilkie Wilkinson, Stan and Sandy—all the mechanics. For me, it was the big time. I had arrived. I remember going to Charterhall for practice on the morning of the first race I ran for them, June 30th, having had three almost sleepless nights beforehand. I was greatly impressed because they wanted to adjust the pedals of the Tojeiro for me. In fact, they wanted to put a footrest in. They actually made one specially for me. Stan and Sandy made one out of alloy and had it riveted into the car in the paddock at Charterhall. I had never experienced anything like this before and it was a great moment of pleasure and excitement. I won the race against very little opposition, except from Tommy Dixon in another Tojeiro Buick—and he was an experienced driver. I was only third in the other race, a Sports Car event won by Jimmy Blumer driving a Cooper Monaco, because I spun very early on at a hairpin bend. But that did not spoil the pleasure of the day. I felt I was being terribly well looked after; and I had won a race for the team."

In twenty-three events that year he collected fourteen firsts, one second and two thirds, and was awarded the Chris Barstow and the Ron Flockhart memorial trophies. Motor racing was now becoming more than a hobby. The crowded weekends of British club racing can produce—indeed have produced—top line drivers year after year. It is a fairly expensive pastime (unless you are lucky enough to find someone who will provide a car for nothing) and you are fortunate if you can cover your traveling and hotel expenses with prize money by the end of the year.

Yet of all his racing career Jackie enjoyed the amateur period the most.

"They were great days. . . . It's one of my regrets that I didn't spend another year of apprenticeship. Charterhall and the nights after the races and all those things were great bun fights—I never really got enough of that. However, things went right for me and so forth. . . ."

At the end of 1963 Jackie got himself a little headline in *Autosport*. "New Lap Record to Jackie Stewart." It was the last meeting of the season at Charterhall, where spectators "saw Jackie Stewart smash the absolute lap record for the circuit with the Ecurie Ecosse Cooper Monaco, finally leaving it at 92.07 mph." Apparently, he "scorched round Charterhall, looking very safe and steady all the way."

43

Early in 1964, a survey of club racing stated that Stewart's name "appeared with monotonous regularity on the top of the results sheets." No one in the country approached his figure of fourteen outright wins, and it became evident that a possible new star had appeared in motor racing. It is interesting, that in the same survey, the man who gets almost as much praise as Jackie is Roy James, one of the Great Train Robbers, now serving a long prison sentence. He had "actually won more club races than anyone else up until his disappearance in August," just keeping his hand in for a more profitable venture!

Interviewed by fellow Scot Graham Gauld in the spring of 1964, a lot of the J. Stewart we now know begins to show up. He talks about *money*, amongst other things, and Gauld adds a kind of apologia to the article, saying that "the purists, or the club drivers of ten years ago might scorn the very frank and almost professional approach to club driving evinced above."

Jackie himself hands out good advice to beginner racing drivers, suggesting that they try to get traveling expenses from the clubs who promote the meetings, and even get a few pounds back in prize money rather than silverware. He states that if he were to choose races, he would go to places like Ouston, where he was able to pick up £50 in one afternoon, or Rufforth, where he earned nearly £30. He points out that his own traveling expenses from Scotland were heavy and that he was relatively lucky in having had a garage business behind him to prepare his E-type in the days before Ecurie Ecosse came along.

He also says that the most important thing he had learned in early races was to consider other people, which he thought difficult when first driving a fast car.

"It is not simply knowing that you can drive fifty miles an hour faster than the next chap; you have got to anticipate his movements."

But perhaps the most interesting part of the interview was what Stewart had to say about the young driver who is trying to break into the sport in a big way.

"He should be a trier, but not overenthusiastic. There is nothing worse for a man considering a driver for the future than to see a bloke hammer a motor car in a rough manner. If a man drives smoothly and well he is not going to be hidden away. He is going to be noticed by the people who count."

That was very true. It is also revealing to read what other people were thinking about Jackie at this time. Jim Clark has this to say in his autobiography, *Jim Clark at the Wheel*.

". . . Jackie Stewart, a young Scottish driver who, I think, has a great deal of ability. Jackie has had a fair amount of experience, having raced a Marcos

Passing a Lotus 23, Stewart in the Cooper Monaco (background) is on his way to another win at Charterhall in 1963.

and an E-type Jaguar and more recently the Ecurie Ecosse Cooper Monaco and Tojeiro Buick. In 1964 he will be driving the Ecurie Ecosse Tojeiro and will also be racing against me in a Cortina Lotus. He is a driver of above average ability."

Michael Kettlewell, a specialist in club racing, regarded him as "underestimated" and points out that in 1963 he scored at least one win at every circuit at which he raced. Another regular reporter states that he "looks forward to Stewart's next appearance." (It is around this same time, incidentally, that one comes across the first obscure mentions of Jochen Rindt, Piers Courage and Jack Oliver.)

In the early Spring of 1964 things began to happen rather quickly. Ecurie Ecosse wanted Stewart to go on driving for them, and Charles Bridges had asked him to drive a Lotus Cortina. Jackie was thus quite happy about the coming season; he had quite enough on his plate for a successful club driver, and the prospect of driving single-seaters had not really dawned on him. He

45

considered them dangerous and still thought of himself as the garage man who went racing for fun on weekends.

As Jackie says, "At that time I wasn't really interested in single seaters . . . my idea of racing was to drive for somebody like John Coombs, and drive only saloon or GT cars."

But he had been "noticed by people who count." Ken Tyrrell, the timber merchant from Surrey, was running the Cooper Formula 3 team at that time and had just lost the promising American driver, Timmy Mayer, in a fatal accident during the Tasman Series. The team was looking for someone to take his place, and Ken, while talking to the Goodwood track manager, had heard about Stewart's equaling the circuit lap record in the Ecurie Ecosse Cooper Monaco and going, as he put it, "like a dose of salts."

Ken telephoned Scotland. Jackie was away shooting, and brother Jimmy took the call. Would Jackie like to come down to Goodwood for a test day in the new Cooper Formula 3 car?

When he heard this message, Jackie was faced with what he recognized as a major decision. He wasn't sure what he wanted to do. He didn't know Ken at all, and he telephoned a lot of people for their opinions on the whole idea, including David Murray and Jim Clark.

"When I put the case, Jimmy said that if I wanted to drive racing cars seriously I *had* to get into single-seater events. He also said that there was no one better to drive for than Ken Tyrrell, if I wanted to get good experience without being pushed too hard."

It was the sort of chance most amateur drivers dream about, and although Jackie was still essentially suspicious, he could hardly do otherwise than agree to try the car at Goodwood. He had reached the point of no return.

That test day stands out for Jackie like a beacon in his career.

"I had the intense pleasure of driving a single-seater car for the first time. This was something I had never done—I had never driven a car that was specially made to go motor racing. This was it. I was not only getting into a fast car, it was a super car—and new, a Cooper T72. It was set up for me by Cooper's Formula One driver at that time, Bruce McLaren, and he was there that day."

To everyone's astonishment, including his own, he was soon lapping faster than Bruce.

"I was very surprised, because I admit that I must have been doing it very blindly. I didn't think I was good at all, I had no false ideas about my ability. I didn't know *how* I'd done it, but I was very pleased that I had."

46

He enjoyed great success in the Jaguar E, winning races at Rufforth, Charterhall, Oulton Park, Crystal Palace and Ouston.

So were John Cooper and Ken Tyrrell. Very early in the session, Ken had looked at his stopwatch with not only surprise but horror at the speed this newcomer was achieving. He called him in and asked him what the hell he was trying to do. After a little lecture he sent Jackie out again, but as he went on lapping even faster, a slow and reluctant smile appeared on Ken's face.

"Ken and John were excited. I could see that. Ken rarely gives you any credit openly. He was never a man to slap you on the back a lot. He was always intensely aware if you were trying too hard, but I could sense he was pleased in spite of the lecture."

John Cooper encouraged Tyrrell to sign up Stewart on the spot. Not that he needed much pushing. As Ken himself says, "There wasn't any doubt in my mind that he was going to be a very fine driver indeed." Jackie had already changed his mind about single-seaters: "It seemed to do everything I wanted it to do." His first taste of driving a machine with precise handling, and the exhilaration of going faster than an established Formula 1 star, must have had a lot to do with his decision to talk business with Ken Tyrrell.

The following day they went to Tyrell's office and Jackie was offered a

47

He became very friendly with the late Jim Clark as they traveled around the world together. Clark felt that Stewart had a great deal of ability and was an above-average driver.

five-year contract to drive for Ken; he was to receive £3000 to sign, and Ken was to take 10 per cent of Stewart's earnings for five years. At this the canny Scotsman in Jackie came to the fore again, alongside the ambitious beginner and the level-headed businessman.

"£3000 was more than I'd hoped to have in my life. I'd been married only eighteen months and I doubt if I had even £50 in the bank. I was comfortable enough, we had a flat and all the things we thought we wanted then, and I was earning about £20 a week. But £3000 . . .

"However, I recognized it as a pretty shrewd deal on Ken's part. I felt that if he, having seen me drive only once, was going to offer me £3000, then there must be more in this racing business than I could see. It was a big, big gamble, but I turned it down. Looking back I'm amazed at myself. I mean, a *Grand Prix* driver wasn't getting that much to sign on with Cooper! I wasn't going to get more anywhere. It was a hell of a decision—but tremendously exciting."

Jackie's instincts proved to be correct, as did Ken's nose for talent! They came to terms over a year's agreement, and Jackie Stewart was, with Warwick Banks, on the Tyrrell BMC Cooper Formula 3 team. It was March 1964.

Rise of a New Star

Two new racing categories came into being in 1964—Formula 2 and Formula 3. Both specified a maximum capacity of 1000cc, but whereas there was no restriction on engine design for F/2 (other than a limit of four cylinders), F/3 power units had to come from production touring cars and were restricted to a single carburetor. There were also all kinds of other limitations on Formula 3 that Formula 2 did not have, and it was obviously intended to make this category as cheap as possible, while F/2 had a certain distinction —a kind of cut-price Formula 1. There was a feeling, an unspoken understanding, that F/3 should be left to amateurs, and it soon became regarded as very much the poor relation—until J. Stewart and K. Tyrrell changed the whole picture!

Ken Tyrrell had been a strong supporter of Formula Junior which had been the forerunner of these new categories, but he soon discovered that promoters and sponsors like fuel companies regarded F/3 as club racing, which could be of no financial interest to them. He was shocked into protesting via the pages of a national magazine. He was receiving no direct support from manufacturers—only a discount from Cooper for buying several

In his first Formula 2 race, driving a Lotus at Clermont-Ferrand, he made the front row of the grid and finished seven seconds behind the winner Denny Hulme.

cars at once. Bonuses on results were restricted to those from component manufacturers. The prize money was ridiculously low.

What Tyrrell wanted was to see Formula 3 get the sort of support from circuit owners and fuel companies that Formula Junior had enjoyed—a state of affairs which had introduced to Formula 1 such drivers as Clark, Surtees, Attwood, Spence, Bandini and Siffert. He wanted to see Formula 3 factory teams, such as exist today, giving the best possible chance of a leg up from club driving to the upper echelons for those who were truly promising. He obviously had Stewart in mind when he said that, and he reflects a good deal of Stewart thinking on the same subject.

Tyrrell's words were printed and heeded, but it took time. And before they were even printed, the first Formula 3 race of the season had been run at Snetterton, in Norfolk, in just about the worst possible weather conditions that even that bleak, flat, ex-airfield circuit has to offer. It was the year's first international meeting in Europe, and a Formula 1 race was won by Innes Ireland in a Lotus Coventry Climax. Jack Brabham won the touring car race in a Ford Galaxie, and Jackie won the Formula 3 event, his first ever single-seater race, by forty-four seconds. It had rained incessantly and heavily for two days—I remember it well, the fields, banks, paddock and approach roads were rapidly oozing together, and it was cold, to boot—but Jackie "just vanished in a cloud of spray," said Ken Tyrrell. It was eight days after his test drive at Goodwood.

Jackie was thrilled, not simply that he'd won his race, but because he'd earned himself £186.

"This I could hardly believe. I had arrived, I had riches. It was all *my* £186. I had no starting money, of course, and I had to pay all my traveling expenses, but it was still damn good."

A week later he was driving at Oulton Park, in Cheshire. First he drove the Red Rose Motors Lotus Cortina and won an exciting scrap by three seconds. Then driving the Ecurie Ecosse Tojeiro Buick he built up a lead of thirty-six seconds in the second race before a timing chain broke. He went on to win a third race, this time in the EE Cooper Monaco, by ten seconds—a varied and successful day!

53

Jackie was getting himself mentioned in the technical press with some enthusiasm, and pictures of him began to appear—in a bewildering array of cars, but always quite recognizably Stewart, who had this early developed a characteristic driving style, smooth and deceptively relaxed.

"That year I drove fifty-three races in twenty-six different cars—I was just driving everything with wheels on."

Two weeks later, again at Oulton Park, the headlines were all for Jim Clark who entered three races and won them all, establishing two lap records in the process. When it came to the Formula 3 event, Jackie Stewart was in the pole position. Just before the start, he found he could not operate the clutch, so he was obliged to switch off, engage first gear and then press the starter when the flag fell. This was pretty shattering for those behind him, and cars went in all directions. It also meant that Jackie was sixth at the end of the first lap, but, almost incredibly, he tore through the field to take the lead on the eighth, to win handsomely and set a new record. His potential was by now obvious to all the motoring pundits.

From that first day at Snetterton Jackie won race after race for Ken Tyrrell in the Cooper BMC. The usual pattern was simply that he led from start to finish—he won eleven out of the thirteen Formula 3 events that he entered.

Not that he never made a mistake. There *are* pictures of Jackie spinning, though not in a Cooper. He seemed to have the measure of that car from his first introduction to it, and his victories were so numerous and by such large margins that people began to complain that he was taking the fun out of racing. (I've heard people say the same thing about Fangio, Stirling Moss, Jim Clark, and, this year, Jackie again!) It was also said that he'd had too easy a time, getting to the top of this particular tree.

Jackie answered critics by saying that it certainly hadn't been all that easy! "I always have to work very hard to get away from the field at the beginning of the race and I always try to maintain this pace if possible." He found that other drivers couldn't match his concentration and pace for as long, and anyway he preferred to race alone. This certainly seems to be the golden rule for the man with his eye on winning Grands Prix—and I suppose any race—get out in front and stay there. One always hears the cry, "Boring," when a driver wins "going away," as Colin Chapman puts it, but when you

look back at the results sheets of the really great World Championship years, you find this psychologically important first lap lead is a major factor.

So Aintree followed Oulton Park, and Silverstone followed Aintree, with Stewart sweeping all before him, and then came Monaco and his greatest triumph to date. As in previous years a Formula Junior race was held on the Grand Prix circuit on the afternoon before the big race, so now it was a Formula 3 race. It is a big event in which to take part, and a lot of prestige attaches to the winner. There are two practice sessions, one on Thursday and the famous, traditional one at dawn on Friday morning. From around 4:00 A.M. one can hear the stirring sound of engines being warmed up all over the Principality, and at 5:30 A.M. the field for the first heat screams up the hill to the Casino. There are few people who can sleep through that!

On Saturday there are two sixteen-lap heats, then a Formula 1 practice and then the F/3 Final, starting just as the shadows grow long over the harbor. This was Jackie's first race abroad. While the star drivers stayed in the grand hotels of Monaco itself, Jackie chose a cheaper and more modest place out in the mountains.

In the first heat he led from start to finish. The second heat went to Silvio Moser in a Brabham who proceeded to win as easily as Stewart had, but took some eight seconds longer to do it. In the final the Swiss driver made a better start than the Scot, and Jackie let him go first into Ste Devote, that notorious corner where enthusiasm can so often get the better part of valor. But on the third lap he took the lead and "proceeded to draw away in his characteristically relaxed style, the stopwatch being the only indication that he was going so much faster than the rest of the field."

He won by seventeen seconds from Moser and was cheered by the Grand Prix stars who had watched the race from their hotel balconies. This was quite a moment for Jackie. These drivers, whom he so revered, were applauding *him*. And, adding to his pleasure, the prize money for Formula 3 at Monaco is worth having!

The next day he acquired a track pass and watched the Grand Prix, taking careful note of how Clark, Hill, Surtees, Brabham, McLaren and company battled with curbs and lampposts, walls and show windows on that demanding circuit. A year later he was to be battling amongst them.

Leading the Rouen Formula 3 race in 1964. He won both Part 1 and Part 2 of the event.

56

Driving a Tojeiro Buick in 1963, he won races at Charterhall, Snetterton and Goodwood.

Gregor Grant, considered one of the greatest authorities on motor racing until his recent death, wrote of the Formula 3 race, "Jackie Stewart showed outstanding skill," and pointed out that this new formula was turning out to be far more exciting than people had anticipated.

In June Jackie earned the headline, "Stewart Supreme"—he won three races in a row at a club meeting at Crystal Palace, first in John Coomb's E-type Jaguar, then in the Chequered Flag Team's Lotus Elan, then with a privately owned XK120. He was nothing if not versatile. And at the end of the month, after winning the Rouen Formula 3 race in the Tyrrell Cooper, and dominating both practice sessions, Bill Gavin wrote of him, "Stewart demonstrated that in less than three months he has already outgrown Formula 3 racing—an undoubted 'natural,' he will surely make his mark in a tougher formula in the three months ahead."

Around British Grand Prix time, someone noticed that Jackie was circulating Brands Hatch in a Formula 1 Lotus during an unofficial practice session, and rumors began to breed. Certainly Colin Chapman already had his eye on this second Scotsman, and Cooper and BRM were also making overtures. When Stewart appeared at Clermont-Ferrand in July driving a Ron Harris Lotus Formula 2 car (he made the front row of the grid and finished seven seconds behind the winner, Denny Hulme), most people assumed he would be forming a Scottish duo with Clark on Team Lotus the following year. If they had known either man at all well, or understood the mentality of a racing driver, I think they would have realized that this was not likely.

Jimmy and Jackie had now become friends, though they were not really close until towards the end of 1965. It was difficult to get close to Jimmy quickly anyway, but there were a number of reasons why it took longer for Jackie to get through to him. For one thing, Jimmy must have recognized a potentially dangerous rival, and nice-natured as he indubitably was, he was also as competitive as any man in the sport. That would have made him a bit cagey. Then there was the basic difference in their natures, Jackie the bouncing extrovert—most of the time—and Jimmy the often unfathomable introvert. The big thing they had in common, their nationality, was the foundation of their growing friendship, for they were both fiercely proud to be Scottish. Later, when Jackie had had a year in Formula 1, and they went out on the Tasman series together, and then to Indianapolis, the bond was cemented by being abroad such a lot—two Scots joined against the world!

But on the same motor racing team? I doubt whether it could have worked, particularly as the rapport between Clark and Colin Chapman was so intense. Colin would not have had patience with Jackie's outspoken, enthusiastic gaiety; Jackie would not have appreciated the often devious politics which surround Colin, after the blunt, down-to-earth Tyrrell. So the rumors went on flying, Jackie went on winning races. He bought himself a bungalow near the Dumbarton garage, and he and Helen moved into their first real home. Now that he was making a living from motor racing, and seemed likely to go on doing so, Jackie stopped taking money from the family business.

"It just couldn't afford to keep us all; there were now three families instead of one, and it was a very small business. I went on working there when I was at home, but I was now, to all intents and purposes, a real professional racing driver."

At the wheel of the Formula 2 Ron Harris Lotus he posted wins at Zolder and at Snetterton.

Helen

In any account of Jackie Stewart's life, his wife, Helen, and their children, Paul and Mark, must form a sizable part. His equable relationship with Helen, and his genuine love for his family and his home, give Jackie an emotional anchorage from which his vitality and ambition can spring renewed.

It can be seen from photographs that Helen is very pretty. She is also graceful, practical and adaptable. She has always possessed these qualities, but only over the last two to three years has Helen Stewart, as a personality in her own right, come to the fore. When I first knew her—the wife of a promising but very new Grand Prix driver (1965)—she was shy, a bit mousy, pregnant and almost silent in company. I saw her as a pale shadow following Jackie, and long before the end of the season she had retired to Scotland to give birth to their first son, Paul.

The following year, with more money and an already attractive dress sense, she made more of an impact. At Monaco, in May 1966, Jackie won his second Grand Prix, and Helen was there to congratulate him, slender as a reed in a beautifully cut trouser suit she had had tailored in London. But she was still very quiet and shy, obviously a bit overawed by the change from their life in Scotland to this noisy, feverish, jet-set existence which is the inescapable lot of Grand Prix racing drivers.

Helen Stewart, now a ravishing strawberry blonde, magazine model-type.

Early in 1967, Mark was born, and I saw little of Helen that year. The Stewarts were living in Clayton House, Dunbartonshire, on the edge of Helensburgh. Jackie describes it as "a super house, very old, terrific character, beautiful inside, a lot of wood, panels and so on. We completely gutted it, except for the woodwork, put in central heating and a complete new kitchen. We had an acre and a half of land, beautifully cared for by a gardener. Leaving it all was the thing we most regretted about leaving Scotland."

But leave they did, finally moving to Switzerland at the end of March 1968; Jackie first, to take a flat until they could find a house, and Helen a couple of weeks later.

Over the last two years I have come to know Helen well and have watched the gradual change from shy Scottish "girl-next-door" to ravishing, strawberry blonde, magazine model-type, sought after by every photographer in Europe. One has only to glance back at the pictures of Helen in the years while Jackie was at BRM to see the difference. Her new appearance has given her greater confidence, plus a spark of fun and a delight in her comfortable, exciting life that she did not have before.

Just before we all left for the Italian Grand Prix 1969, at which Jackie clinched his World Championship title, Helen and I sat in Jackie's study, talking, while the men, for once, were outside looking after the children—ostensibly. We switched on the tape recorder, ignored the yells from the garden and chatted until finally interrupted by Jackie, who burst in and said, "Haven't you finished yattering *yet*?" I've left our conversation almost exactly as it was on the tape, and let Helen speak for herself.

E. H. Do you feel fairly at home here now?

H. S. When I first came out I was quite nervous at the thought of a new country—I'd moved before, many times, but this time it was a big move, and I'd no idea if I'd like it or not. I didn't really know anyone, apart from Jo and Marianne Bonnier.

Of course, when I came out, Jimmy [Clark] had just been killed, that weekend. I came over on the Tuesday after. I arrived, met Jackie at the

Wedding day for Jackie and Helen, 1962.

65

Born John Young Stewart, Jackie was raised in this house in Dumbartonshire, Scotland.

airport, and he sort of said, hello, goodbye and left me. He went on to Jimmy's funeral and stayed over there for a few days. So I was really on my own. I *did* get homesick then. Our best friend had just been killed and I didn't ever want to see a motor race again at that time. I had a strange language to contend with, and I wasn't even in my own home, I was living in a furnished flat which I wasn't used to. Particularly with children, it drives you crazy if you aren't used to it. But . . . somehow you seem to get hold of yourself and get on.

E. H. Quite brave, though.

H. S. I don't know if it's bravery, but I think it was then I began to change.

E. H. Had you been very dependent on Jackie prior to that? You always seemed to be.

H. S. Yes, I think I was more dependent on him than I am now. I remember the days when I used to be absolutely petrified if someone were coming to

"Don't worry, darling, you can't win them all," Helen seems to be saying after Jackie's retirement in one of his early Tasman Series races.

dinner. I would never even *dream* of entertaining if Jackie was away. And even when he was there, I never said a word. I sat there, served a meal, and that was it. I might as well have been a servant.

E. H. That wasn't just with foreigners, you mean with anyone?

H. S. Yes, even people at home, in Scotland. It helped having Nina and Jochen [Rindt] move in down the road this year, although they were away a lot in the early months. I must say I was glad when Nina came. She thinks the same way as I do, fortunately, and we get on very well together, and so do Jackie and Jochen.

E. H. How is your French coming along? Are you still going for lessons?

H. S. (Bashfully) No. I haven't got time, we've been away so much.

E. H. Will you go on with them in the winter?

(Guilty giggle from Helen.)

E. H. No, I can see you won't.

H. S. I mean to take skiing lessons in the winter!

E. H. But you did get on well with French while you were at it.

H. S. I did, yes, it was meant to be a crash course, lasting five weeks. But I took two months over it! I learned quite a lot, but I learnt more being amongst the people and speaking, you know, just picking things up. I've found out more like that than from the lessons.

E. H. Jackie has never said how you met. In fact, I've never got round to asking him.

H. S. First of all I met him when I was sixteen, twelve years ago, and he was seventeen. I was introduced to him by a mutual friend, a boy friend of a girl friend of mine. He was coming down to meet *his* girl friend, with Jackie, to meet another girl. On a blind date. This other girl was a friend of mine also. But it so happened that I was sitting talking to the other boy's girl friend when Jackie arrived with him. And the girl who he was *supposed* to take out was sitting at another table. I hope you can follow all that. It was the sort of place where young people gather, for a coffee—a coffee shop in Helensburgh, where I was born. Jackie and I started talking, and eventually I thought, "I'd better go and tell this girl if she is going out with him she

The Stewart lounge should be called a "salon" for it has a decidedly French atmosphere.

70

ought to come over and sit next to him." So I went and told her that, and she took one look at him and said, "I don't want to go out with *him*!" I was flabbergasted. Jackie at that time was a very different person from now. He was the same height, but a very thin person, with spots on his face. And honestly, no girl would have looked twice.

E. H. Why did you?

H. S. Well, when I was introduced to him he started talking to me, and the funny thing was, I liked his voice. And he was very well-mannered, which was a thing I'd never been used to. I mean, sixteen and just left school, I didn't really know many boys. He was the same sort of *character* he is now, though he's even better. I just enjoyed talking to him, I found him very interesting. Plenty of vitality. It wasn't love at first sight on either part, nothing like that. We went out together occasionally. I think Jackie was more fond of me than I was of him at that time. Fortunately I realized that liking him was one thing, but I didn't know what it was like to be in love with anyone, never having experienced it. So I suggested we split up for a while, which was a good thing, because he went out with other girls, and I went out with other boys—I think it's a thing you have to do. I don't think you can go steady with one person at that age. Although Jackie had mentioned marriage, I never thought I would marry him. I'd always reckoned to marry somebody tall, dark and handsome, the usual girl's idea, but it never works that way.

Anyhow, about eight months later I met him again. It was the funniest thing. I'll always remember it. I can remember *exactly* when I felt I was in love with him. I was nineteen at the time, and he came walking into the same coffee shop.

E. H. And it all happened!

H. S. Yeah! But you can't go up to somebody and say, I want you to take me out again, that's the sort of thing I'd never do. But he must have felt the same way, because—well, it was a bit silly, really—I had a ring, and he took it and wouldn't give it back to me, and being a typical woman I got up and walked out and said, "All right if you won't give it back to me, too bad, I'm going home." So he followed me, and I tried to act as if I were annoyed,

71

but I wasn't annoyed at all really! He had a fabulous red Austin Healey at that time, and he followed me in this car with my ring. He asked me if I'd like a lift, and I said, No, I'd walk on my own. But he said, "Come on, don't be silly, let me give you a lift." Of course all the time I wanted to, but I didn't want to seem too eager. Anyway, he took me home, and that was the start of it, all over again—but completely different. Grown up. We were engaged about eighteen months later and married two years later, and we've been married seven years. We've had two children, and four homes. Each home has gone up and up, bigger and bigger. It's amazing how your life changes. When we were first married he was only racing about twice a year, and there was no prospect of his ever becoming a professional racing driver.

E. H. When he began to race more, did you worry about it or didn't you think he'd ever do it seriously?

H. S. He was only doing club racing. As far as I was concerned it was only a hobby. It was something to do on a Sunday. All our friends used to go together. I never even timed Jackie—I used to sit in a car and read the Sunday newspapers. And everyone thought I was a queer bird! I wasn't the slightest bit interested. I'm still not, I don't know the first thing about a car. I'm just glad when he finishes and disappointed when he doesn't finish.

E. H. Do you get this feeling, when they break down in the race and come back to the pits—It's almost a feeling of relief that they are safe, even if they are disappointed?

H. S. Oh, yes, I do. It's the most horrible feeling that I can think of when you're sitting waiting, and nobody has any idea why they haven't come round. I never think Jackie's had an accident, I never think that at all. At Spa, for instance, in 1966, I think I was the last person to know he'd had an accident. Graham told me eventually that he'd broken his shoulder, but I thought he was quite okay. That was the first I knew that *anything* had happened to him.

E. H. It was a good thing you didn't know, there's nothing whatever you can do.

H. S. No. There had been other reports, but you wouldn't have known anything for sure. I was told that he was standing by the road. At least, there were two drivers standing by the road beside a BRM. Of course, so many

72

drivers went off on that lap. Fifteen cars started, seven came round on the first lap.

Sometimes I get terribly fed up with it. Up until this year I didn't really go very much. Last year I went to all the Grands Prix, but I didn't go to the Formula 2 races.

E. H. But now he is Champion—touch wood—you will be invited to many more non-racing functions. That's another thing—do you get as upset as I do when people anticipate the outcome of a race, like commentators saying several laps before the end, "This is the first race he's won this year," or the third or whatever, long before? . . .

H. S. Yes, I hate that. John Whitmore came up to me at Silverstone, about six laps from the end of the British Grand Prix and said, "We're going to leave now, Jackie's got it in the bag, anyway." And I thought, "Oh, God, I wish he wouldn't say such things." I think he realized I was annoyed. It's a very personal thing, and I don't want people to think I'm stupid, or superstitious.

E. H. No, it's more like tempting providence. Maybe that *is* superstition. Yes, we'll have to admit it, Helen, we're superstitious.

H. S. Yes, I suppose so. I don't like to offend the other person, I don't really know how to handle it. Whether to be downright rude, or just ignore them.

E. H. I should look into the distance and pretend to be doing something else.

H. S. That's what I do. I just sit there with my head down, and I know there are people standing there looking up, just waiting for a moment to say something, and I ignore them. I look as if I'm in a complete trance! They probably think, "Gormless, she's gone to sleep!"

E. H. I'm sure that's the best way to handle it, then you can't offend anyone. Changing the subject a bit, do you mind being away from Scotland?

H. S. No, not really. There are times when I wish I could see more of my parents, but my home is here now. I don't miss Scotland as a place. I went back about two weeks ago, and I must say it was nice to see everyone. The town of Helensburgh gave me a feeling of being at home, but that's natural if you've been brought up somewhere, and lived there for twenty-seven years.

Would you buy a used car from this man? Helen doesn't like it quite so long but really doesn't see what the fuss is all about.

I must say I don't think I would like to live there now, because of Jackie doing so well. Life would be unbearable—it was getting that way before we left. People coming up in the street to talk about him, and so on. I think it would be worse there than here. I don't think they'd come up to the house, as they do here, but out shopping they would stare and come up and say things, good and bad. It doesn't matter what you do, people say bad things. Once this year I came up from the basement and found five people standing in the hall! They had just walked in. It was very difficult to get them to go away.

E. H. What are your best times now, since you came to live in Switzerland?

H. S. I like staying at home with Jackie best, though we very, very seldom get the chance to be completely alone. When we get back he always has things to do in Geneva, and I have things to do in the house anyway, all the washing and ironing and repacking, maybe for going away again two days later. But I like to get everything done the day after I get back, which normally gives me one day free—I have to let Margaret (the Scottish House-keeper-Nannie) off. And I try to cram the whole lot into one day. Tomorrow I'm going to be alone but Jackie is playing golf so I shall go into Geneva. Then Thursday we go to Deauville for talks with the Matra people. There was a time, four months in 1968, when we weren't alone at all, not for a day.

E. H. Do you ever make decisions at home or does Jackie? I suppose he has to, as it all revolves around racing.

H. S. If I arranged something he wouldn't do it anyway! When he's at home, I couldn't suddenly say I want some people I know up for dinner, he wouldn't want that, he'd want his friends; it's very much a man's world. Jackie loves to entertain—so do I, but there are times when you like to be alone. After Deauville it's back here and on to Monza.

E. H. Then Canada.

H. S. I'm not going to Canada, or any of the transatlantic races. If it were possible to go over and go on from Canada to Watkins Glen and then to Mexico, having a real holiday in between that would be fine, but it isn't possible. Jackie's time is all taken up with broadcasts and TV shows and so on, promotions, etc., at which I'd only be trotting around like the cow's tail, if you'll excuse the expression!

E. H. What will you do?

H. S. I don't know. I've been rushing around so much, I've been dying to be on my own, but when I am I suppose I shan't know what to do. As a matter of fact, Nina and I are both looking forward to being on our own for a bit. When the men are here there's never a dull moment, people coming, people phoning.

E. H. Perhaps you'll go into Geneva and have a clothes-buying orgy.

H. S. I have a dress allowance which has to last me for a year. You know,

76

if I didn't, I could go into a shop and just buy and buy, and never stop, or I could go in and think I can't have that, I might not be able to afford it. If you know exactly what you've got, you know what you can spend. We house-keep on a budget too.

E. H. That's a bit unusual for people whose money comes in in large lumps.

H. S. Well, it's not always going to come in in large lumps, therefore it's best to know exactly where you stand all the time. It is very hard to budget —you can't tell when you're going to have people to entertain. Or suddenly I might want something, a piece of furniture, maybe. Sometimes it is very difficult to justify saying I *can't* afford something when I know very well that I can. But it doesn't come into the budget. It is very easy to go on, spend, spend, spend, when you know you've got it. We have both been very sensible with money. When we were first married, although we had everything we wanted, we lived from week to week, in a flat, on about £9 a week.

E. H. If Jackie doesn't win, or something goes wrong, is he disappointed, or irate about it, or philosophical?

H. S. Well, obviously he gets disappointed at times, more so if the car breaks down or, as at Spa, if he runs out of petrol, but he doesn't get too upset about it. That race is over, on to the next one, next week. He doesn't brood on it. It's finished. There are more things to do.

E. H. Is he difficult on race morning, as some drivers are—one doesn't dare speak to some of them.

H. S. Oh, I'll speak to Jackie if I have something to say, but I won't talk just for the sake of talking. He's very good, but I do know he prefers to be on his own. He likes to lie and read in the morning, and I don't mind. I like to lie and sleep anyway. We have breakfast as normal, then get ready and go to the track. He's very even-tempered. (At that moment Jackie came in to get a book, knocked something over and swore bad-temperedly! We laughed a good deal and he couldn't understand why.)

E. H. His hair—has he a good reason for growing it so long? If it's a secret, switch off the tape recorder.

H. S. No, there's no secret, it's something that just happened. Last year he broke his wrist in practice in Madrid. The weather was fabulous here in Switzerland and all he wanted to do was just lie out in the sunshine. So he didn't want to go to a barber, and I cut his hair, trimmed it at the back. I didn't even touch the sideburns. And they got bushier and bushier and I looked at him and said, "You know, I rather like you like that." To me it was "sexy." It made me look twice at him. He said, "Do you think I should keep them that way?" and I said, "Yes," but I thought he ought to try to grow it down to a certain length and comb it forward. Anyhow, October last year he went to California and had it cut by Jay Sebring, and it was all combed forward, exactly the way I'd told him to do it. The fact that he'd

Helen with Jim Clark and Jackie at Zandvoort in 1967. By this time Jimmy and Jackie had become close friends.

been to this world-famous hairdresser was something—he respected his opinion. He's been back once or twice to have it cut. He didn't go all the way to Los Angeles just to have a haircut, he happened to be there. He hasn't been back for a long time, and he didn't find anyone he liked in London, and he just hasn't had the time. Now Jay Sebring is dead . . . and it got longer and longer. I must say I don't like it quite so long—slightly shorter. It gets in the way a bit. I can't understand why it is such a topic of conversation.

E. H. I think it is because it makes him look like the people the middle-aged, middle-class, middle of the road people dislike so much—they wonder what he is protesting about!

H. S. Have you ever heard the record of the show *HAIR*?

E. H. Yes.

H. S. One particular song in it, it says "What does it matter if you have your hair long, Christ had his hair long." I know it probably looks odd with present day clothes, but they wore it long in the sixteenth and seventeenth century—I like long hair. It is just convention really, that men get their hair cut. I think some people do have it long in order to rebel against convention, but it's a matter of personal choice. Some people think it's dirty—I do know that Jackie washes it every day, because he likes it to lie a certain way. My mother hates it, she goes on and on. But my mother goes on about me anyway, she's never changed. She's on to me about mini-skirts and about having hair hanging round my face all the time. The reason I grew mine . . . I used to feel that as I was married and a mother I ought to have my hair short. And then I felt I was beginning to look just like a mother and nothing else.

E. H. Then the new Helen took over!

H. S. Yes! Because I wanted to look more like a girl friend for Jackie than a staid wife. It didn't suddenly happen, but I decided it was too soon to

become a matron. I think Nina had a lot to do with it. Clotheswise, anyway. We shop at the same places in Geneva.

E. H. Do you ever row?

H. S. No, we've never had a row since the day we got married. We've had differences of opinon, but . . .

E. H. He doesn't throw things, or anything like that?

H. S. No. It's absolutely fantastic, we just get on so well together we seem to synchronize. There are times when I might rebel against something, because he's a typical man at times. Egotistical. I rebel in some little way. If my mother wanted me to do something and I wouldn't, there was *no way* she could get me to do it. I'm still the same.

E. H. Stubborn.

H. S. Yes. We both are, but Jackie's much better than I am. More flexible. I do get annoyed with him at times, but it only lasts about two minutes, because he just needs to look at me and I laugh.

E. H. Marvelous. I hope it stays that way.

H. S. So do I!

Into the Big League

It was typical of Stewart's clear sense of where he was going, and what would be the best all-round thing to do in any situation, that he chose to join BRM for the 1965 season. He had made up his mind and announced his decision by September 1964.

"I joined the team to get first-class experience," he says. "A team where I could learn at my own pace—and learn from someone like Graham Hill. I knew I would be well looked after too, and not be rushed."

It was a well-thought-out step in a long series of such steps evolved by a man with a needle-sharp planner's mind. Maybe, as Jackie says, he was just lucky in the way things happened to him—you certainly need a lot of luck in motor racing, and I don't mean that in the crossed-fingers-in-case-of-accidents kind of way. You have to be the right man, in the right car, on the right tires, in the right place, at the right time to get the best breaks. But some people get all the breaks and then amount to nothing more than a nine-day wonder. It takes determination, foresight and, most of all, natural talent to shoot through the apprenticeship period like a meteor, as Stewart did.

Before the end of the season, Jackie had scored his eleventh Formula 3 victory out of thirteeen in Ken Tyrrell's Cooper BMC and was third to Brabham and Clark in the Gold Cup F/2 meeting at Oulton Park—they were the only three drivers on the same lap at the finish. Finishing on the same lap as two World Champions must have been a thrill for Jackie at the time, but he's never mentioned it. Maybe it all seems very long ago.

On the strength of his Formula 2 drives in the Ron Harris Lotus (and because Jim Clark had slipped a disc snowballing in Italy!) Jackie was offered a Formula 1 Lotus for the Rand Grand Prix at the Kyalami circuit in South Africa in December. It was a two-heat aggregate-time type of race and, for Jackie, full of drama. He put up fastest time in Jimmy's car and was on the pole for the first heat—then broke a drive shaft on the line. Graham Hill, who had not practiced and started from the back row, drove past everyone to win. In the second heat, Stewart did precisely the same thing. The broken drive shaft had been replaced, and he started from the back of a long two-by-two grid.

"It was most impressive," says a reporter, "to watch Stewart set about his task so competently, and after a perfect start he disposed of one car after another as though they were standing still."

It was now time to move into the big league. Christmas and New Year in South Africa means warmth, swimming, parties and the Grand Prix (at least, it did till they moved the GP to March). On January 1, 1965, two Scots celebrated Hogmanay, one by winning—Jimmy Clark led the race from start to finish—and the other, Jackie Stewart, by driving in his first-ever Grand Prix and collecting his first Championship point by finishing sixth. Jackie was now Graham Hill's teammate, an experience which was to prove invaluable to him, and for which he never forgets to thank Graham on every suitable occasion. His praise and his gratitude are deeply sincere.

"From my point of view he was the perfect teammate—a man who, above all, was one of the fairest men I have ever raced with. He could have been very difficult—I came in as a real greenhorn, and I was going quite quickly. He could have made life difficult for me, but he never did. Certainly, he was getting the best engine of the two, but it was his right to have it as he was Number One driver and had been there five full seasons. I was a very new boy, but this did not worry me at all. Graham's assistance was very valuable, and he gave it in such a way that I shall always respect him for it. I don't think I'd have been able to learn so much on any other team, bar none."

Of that first outing with the BRM, Jackie remembers that he was very

His first Formula 1 victory was at Silverstone in 1965, the (non-Championship) International Trophy.

At the French Grand Prix he was second to Clark for the second time in 1965, his first full year in Formula 1. He finished third in point standings behind Clark and Hill.

pleased with the handling, but thought that the Lotus he had driven in the Rand GP was a bit quicker off the mark. He regarded Jimmy and Lotus as a virtually unbeatable combination, and while not for a second regretting signing with BRM he genuinely thought the Lotus a faster car and Jimmy the best driver in the business.

For these reasons he was quite satisfied to take second place behind Jimmy several times that year, though looking back now, he is a little surprised that his now insatiable will to win was sublimated at that time. He admits he used to think a lot about why Jimmy was quicker, why he was beating everyone, and that he would have liked to have tried his skill against Clark's in an identical car. (This is the normal reaction of any racing driver to the man who is always winning, and I have watched a number of very expressive faces during 1969, Grand Prix drivers and constructors who were wondering just what Stewart had that they didn't!)

A great deal was expected of Stewart in his first year of Formula 1, at least from the press and public. In fact, a great deal began to be expected

At Goodwood in 1965 he put his BRM on the pole position. He shared a new lap record with Clark before retiring with engine trouble.

of all "second" drivers. It was no longer enough to have one star and one novice (or an also-ran) on a team; the second driver, shrewd team managers were beginning to realize, ought to be capable of winning races. As well as Jackie, Mike Spence and Jochen Rindt had now come into Formula 1 and all three had enough "tiger" in them to be up there with the Champions and to hell with team positions.

As if to prove the point, the first big Formula 1 race of the season in the U.K., the Race of Champions at Brands Hatch in March, was a triumph for Spence and Stewart, who finished first and second after Clark crashed and Hill's engine died on him.

At the Goodwood Easter meeting an even more obvious storm-warning was raised—Jackie took the pole position in his BRM with a 1:19.8 lap, while alongside him on the front row were Graham Hill and Jim Clark, each credited with 1:20.6. Jimmy won the race and Graham was second, as things turned out, because it was Jackie's turn to be defeated by engine trouble, but he managed to share a new lap record with Clark before retiring.

Stewart leads John Surtees during the Race of Champions at Brands Hatch in 1965. He finished second to Mike Spence.

Then, at Silverstone in May, came the climax to Jackie's extraordinary rise to fame. He won the International Trophy race.

"It was my first Formula One victory, and it was a big moment. I'd had a really good dice with John Surtees, which was a pleasure, because he was the reigning World Champion and I had only just started. The rest of that year was also very satisfying."

I should think so! Jackie finished third at Monaco; second in the Belgian GP, fifth in the British, second in the Dutch, retired in the German and won the Italian. He ended his first year at BRM third in the World Championship point standings behind Clark and Hill.

The Italian Grand Prix, which should have been such a high spot, was spoiled for him because Graham had gone slightly off-course on the second to last lap and Jackie was worried that it had been his fault, as they were traveling in very close company at the time, which is nothing unusual at Monza.

"Graham had come up to me afterwards and said it wasn't my fault, but I wasn't sure whether he was just being nice to me, so as not to spoil my big occasion. Later on we all sat round at dinner and watched the race on television, the whole team—it was a tense moment. Fortunately, it showed that he had been slightly behind me when he went off, so it cleared my conscience. But during the time I should have been most elated I had this funny little feeling inside me that didn't quite allow my excitement to bubble over. So, although it was my first Grand Prix win, it was somewhat spoiled.

"In fact, the feeling of anti-climax was so strong that when I won at Monte Carlo the following May, I genuinely felt it to be my first Grand Prix. I had forgotten Monza. It wasn't until I was halfway round the circuit on that little bus thing that takes you on a lap of honor that I realized it was the second."

Of that first season, 1965, a great deal was written. Jackie's name was not only linked with Clark's by reason of their nationality but because Jimmy's fellow countryman "looks like he's following in the master's wheel tracks."

Second place to Clark in the Belgian Grand Prix at Spa pleased Jackie most of all.

"I remember getting a great kick out of it, because we were both Scottish

89

He beat teammate Graham Hill to record his first Grand Prix victory at Monza in 1965.

and we both made the front page of every Scottish newspaper together—"First and Second for Scotland!"—that sort of thing. And it was a difficult race, in streaming rain, and we beat the others fair and square; in fact we lapped everyone at least once."

Jimmy had the Championship all sewed up by the end of the German GP and people were saying exactly what they said of Stewart in 1969—that he'd taken the fun out of the rest of the season. This was nonsense then as it is now. Each race is another challenge to these men, and they will give everything they have to whatever scrap they happen to be engaged in. There have been times when teams, and occasionally drivers, have retired from the fray after settling the title, but those days are long gone. As we witnessed this past year, the Canadian, the American and the Mexican Grands Prix were as hard-fought and as exciting as any of 1969, with the possible exception of Monza, and don't imagine that Jackie Stewart was anything but frustrated and annoyed at being put out of the Canadian by Jackie Ickx's overenthusiasm! A race is to be run, and a race is to be won, if at all possible, and the more the merrier.

When he finished second to Clark in the 1965 Belgian Grand Prix, they made the front page of every Scottish newspaper together: "First and Second for Scotland!"

At the end of 1965, David Phipps wrote in his annual *Autocourse,* "One of the big events of the year was the arrival of Jackie Stewart in Formula 1. During the previous three years it had become obvious that Clark, Hill, Gurney and Surtees were the elite of Grand Prix racing, but it was not long before Stewart proved to be every bit as fast as any of them—with the possible exception of Clark. . . . His most remarkable achievement was probably his incredible 8 min. 26.1 sec. practice lap at the Nürburgring, which he did after only a few laps of familiarization. In the race he made one of his rare mistakes, put a wheel off the road and bent a wishbone: It must be nice for the other drivers to know that he is at least human!"

So Stewart went into 1966 with this accolade, among many others, giving him at last some real confidence in his ability. Because of his bouncy walk, the readiness and ease with which he talks to absolutely anyone and his almost complete absence of "temperament," most people assume that he is not only confident but conceited—"cocky" has been the word most often used against him. He is not conceited. He is thoughtful, sensitive, far-sighted and clear thinking. He will always listen to two sides of a question and decide for himself after deliberation. He is cautious, a natural characteristic of the Scots, and he is well aware that, though at the moment he is "the man to beat," as Stirling Moss puts it, there are several other drivers who can be as good, given the right circumstances. One, his neighbor and friend Jochen Rindt, is often faster.

Jackie never feels confident about a race beforehand, even if he is in the region of two seconds quicker than anyone else and the car is perfect. He never feels in any way "superior."

Therefore the praise he received for his driving in 1965 carried him into the following year, his second with BRM, on the crest of a wave.

Triumph and Disaster

The Grand Prix season of 1966 was expected to be a bit muddled, because of the change in Formula 1 from 1½ liters to 3 liters. It was not until well on in the year that the 3-liter engines came into their own and began to show their real capabilities. Apart from the battles between cars—there were eight factory teams competing in most races—and between drivers, there was just as much at stake between the rival tire companies. For Dunlop it was their lowest ebb, with only two wins in the early part of the season; by the Mexican Grand Prix not a single car was using their tires. The big American companies, Goodyear and Firestone, after a shaky start and a lot of nagging from constructors, had taken over Grand Prix racing and were in the ascendant for two years.

At BRM the H16 engine had been evolved, a beautiful design but very complicated. Although it appeared in practice at Monaco, Spa and Reims, it was beset by a variety of problems which have still not been satisfactorily cured. Lotus, too, had arranged to use BRM engines upon the withdrawal of Coventry Climax from racing, and pending the development of the Cosworth Ford. In fact, the first BRM H16 to finish a race that year was in Jimmy Clark's car when he won the U.S. Grand Prix at Watkins Glen!

1967 was a pretty dismal year for Stewart and BRM with the car dropping out
of one race after the other and only placing second in the Belgian and third
in the French Grands Prix.

Early in the year BRM raced their 1965 cars with 1916cc versions of the
1½-liter V8 engine in the Tasman Series and got off to a good start by "clean-
ing up." Jackie won four races and gained a second and a fourth place in two
others to take the Tasman title, while Graham Hill also won two and Dickie
Attwood one. It was in one of these cars that Jackie won the Monaco Grand
Prix, while Graham Hill was third in another.

Jackie was jubilant about winning at Monaco. Most people had expected
the Ferraris with their new 3-liter engines and their two great drivers, Surtees
and Bandini, to dominate the meeting, but though Stewart and Surtees had a
nose to tail duel for the first fourteen laps and Bandini finished second, it was a
disappointing race for everyone except BRM.

"It was a real occasion, I enjoyed every moment of it. I think to win at

Jackie started 1966 by winning the first Grand Prix of the season. Here
Louis Chiron gives him the checkered flag at Monaco.

95

Monte Carlo is a marvelous thing anyway, but I had led the race the previous year until I made a mistake, and it was nice because of that, too."

There was also the fact that by now Jackie was getting a taste for gracious living and for all the good things that money can buy. He was making his first attempt at Indianapolis that month, and had rushed back by jet to Monaco after qualifying, won the GP, jetted back to Indy, and almost won that too. Jackie lists it as the third biggest disappointment of his life.

He was driving a Lola, the Bowes Seal Fast Special and Graham Hill was in John Mecom's Lola, the American Red Ball Special. It was a weird race. "500" devotees will remember it as the year of the multiple pileup, when the tremendous climax which is always reached as the pace car slopes off the track and leaves the monsters streaking on was followed by perhaps the biggest fright they've ever had at Indy, and that's saying something. One car hit the wheel of another forward of midfield, and in an instant sixteen cars were spinning, crashing and flying to pieces. Eleven of them were demolished, including A. J. Foyt's and Dan Gurney's. Spectators were injured by flying metal, but miraculously, no one, not even a driver, was seriously hurt.

It took an hour and a half to clear up the mess and get the rest of the field restarted. Among those who had avoided the drama were Clark, Hill, Stewart, Mario Andretti, Lloyd Ruby, Roger McCluskey and Jim McElreath. Even after the first disaster there were crashes, blown engines and yellow lights. . . . It was not the best of races.

With a hundred miles still to go Jackie was out in front and it seemed certain that he would win. He was almost a lap ahead of Jim Clark in second place. Suddenly, with only nine laps to go—a little more than twenty miles— the Lola pulled onto the grass near the northeast turn. The oil pressure had dropped and the engine seized.

"To find myself in the lead at Indianapolis . . . I don't think I've got over the shock yet. I knew there had been a lot of trouble ahead of me, but I didn't think I'd been going at that sort of pace. I remember passing people— I suppose I must have passed Jimmy too. I can't remember, but it was a good dice for quite a few laps; Jimmy and I were understanding each other very well. When I walked back—as Graham went on to win—I had an ovation

Denny Hulme congratulates Jackie on having qualified for the 1967 Indy "500." Stewart was later bumped from the field but came back to qualify another car.

Jackie returned in 1967 to defend his Tasman Series title, but the combination of his good friend Jimmy Clark and his Lotus was too much to stop.

such as I had never heard before. I felt very philosophical about dropping out, because I had received a bigger reception than I had ever got in motor racing before, and because I treated the thing well, I was applauded even more. I was pleased, not just about the crowd, but because I had led the race, and I had shown everyone that I *could* win it.

"As for the money—well, it is as important to me as to the American drivers, maybe more so. I must have lost $130,000, or thereabouts. Receiving the Rookie of the Year award gave me a boost, but I had a small area of depression coming in that was put back a day or so. I must admit that two days after the race I was bitterly disappointed that I hadn't won it. It was sad; but not all that sad, because I had been satisfied with my personal performance, and that is important."

Stewart, here leading the Phil Hill/Mike Spence Chaparral which won the race, co-drove this factory Ferrari with Chris Amon to second place in the 1967 BOAC 500.

The following weekend the Grand Prix circus went to Spa for the Belgian GP. Jackie, still in the 2-liter BRM, was first on the track when practice started and set a good lap time of 3:41.5, which was four seconds faster than the unofficial circuit record. Surtees, however, in good form in the Ferrari, soon knocked another second off that, and on the second day produced a shattering 3:38 which no one was able to beat. Jochen Rindt was second fastest with 3:41.2 and Jackie made the third man on the front row.

On Saturday night the hot weather broke up into storms. Rain was expected on Sunday, and those who needed to had changed tires accordingly, Ferraris back to Dunlops and Clark to wet-weather Firestones. But no one dreamed of what was in store for the drivers as they set off on their first lap on what appeared to be a dry track.

There were fifteen starters. Of these, only seven came around at the end of the lap. On the far side of the 8¾-mile circuit, a torrential rain shower had turned the track into a river. Bonnier, Spence, Hulme and Siffert all spun off at Burnenville and were out of the race, but farther down the road conditions were even worse, and the BRMs of Stewart, Hill and Bondurant all went off there. Stewart had aquaplaned at 150 mph, gone off the road and knocked down a couple of walls and smashed into a telegraph post. He was trapped in his car, which was rapidly filling up with thirty-two gallons of fuel. The monocoque had wrapped itself around Jackie's legs so he couldn't get out, and the ignition could not be switched off because the dashboard had been destroyed.

It was very lucky for Jackie that Graham Hill had spun off at the same place and saw his teammate's car through the curtains of rain. Even so, Jackie lay for thirty-five minutes in his fuel bath, which could, at any second, go up in a ball of flame.

"The accident itself doesn't exist in my mind at all. I remember going off the road, but I don't remember crashing into anything. I remember Graham getting out of his car and running over and trying to get me out, with Bob Bondurant arriving slightly later. Graham is a very cool person under every strain and I couldn't have wanted anybody better than Graham at that time, though even he was a bit tweaked up. I remember that he tried to push the monocoque out with his hands, and I must admit I had a horrible fear because of the petrol. I couldn't move. I knew something had broken up around my

He had worked his way from twenty-ninth to third in the 1967 Indy "500" when his engine blew, putting him out in the same place as the previous year.

shoulder, but I couldn't get my legs out because the steering wheel was all tangled round me.

"Graham had to go and borrow spanners from the tool kit of a spectator's car to get me out, and of course, it was a long business. After that BRM put spanners inside the cockpits of the cars, with instructions in the language of every country we visit. I still have this done today, in Ken's cars."

Strangely enough, Jackie looks back on that horrific day and recalls something pleasant about it. After Graham had lifted him out of the wrecked car, taken him to a barn and stripped off his fuel soaked clothing, an ambulance eventually came out to collect him. (Spa is a long circuit, with many stretches of wooded country and very sparsely spaced marshals. It often takes a long time for news of any kind to get back to the pit area. The only helicopter that came over while Jackie was awaiting deliverance was one which was being used for the filming of Frankenheimer's *Grand Prix* and that didn't stop!)

"It was when I had been treated a little—I had broken my collarbone and dislocated my shoulder, and cracked some ribs, but the petrol burns were hurting most—and I had been put in an ambulance to go to hospital in Liege. Louis Stanley, Helen and Jimmy were there, and Jimmy was looking after Helen very well because she was a bit upset. She hadn't heard anything about the accident till long after it happened. Louis Stanley was looking after me, and I can remember him telling me that they had arranged a jet to fly me that night from Liege to London. They had arranged it so quickly . . . I remember thinking, 'Oh, good!' I was absolutely scared stiff of staying in a hospital on the continent, and it was such a relief to know I was going back to Britain. I was talking all the time. I had been given jabs of this and that, and I didn't know how badly I was hurt but I knew they were worried that I might have a back injury or something. It was silly, I suppose, but oh! the tremendous relief to know I was going home!"

It was while he was lying in the hospital after this accident, and during his convalescence, that Jackie formed some very clear and determined ideas about safety on the motor racing circuit. He recalled his brother's crashes and the unnecessary way in which lives were lost every year on the track for want of a complete re-think on the whole subject.

He has been much criticized for his safety-conscious outlook and his influence on the Grand Prix Drivers Association. Some sections of the press have attacked him in print for what they call "emasculating the sport." If they mean by this that they would prefer to see drivers killed, when the provision of a few feet of steel barrier or a safety harness could save them, then their mentality is beyond my comprehension. It is largely thanks to Jackie that some of the most dangerous places on the world's race tracks—for spectators as well as drivers—have been made less lethal. Graham Hill and Jochen Rindt would almost certainly have been killed in the Spanish Grand Prix of 1969 if the circuit had not been lined recently with Armco barrier, and wire fences put up to keep the crowds safe.

Jackie is always one of the first to wear the latest and best in helmets, overalls, underwear and seat belts, and he explains his reasons in his lucid, commonsense way.

"I am a professional racing driver and I enjoy it, but I realize that if I drive regularly for maybe ten years, I would be a fool to think I wouldn't have an accident in that time, whether due to my error or to a mechanical failure. If I did not prepare myself for an accident by using the best helmet, the best thermal underwear, the best fireproof overalls and so on, I would be irresponsible. I want to survive. I want to live, preferably to a good old age. The only way I am likely to achieve that is by taking proper precautions. And if I can help perhaps by suggesting that a fence or a barrier be placed there which might not only save my life but the lives of young, novice drivers, I think I am doing a service to them and to the sport.

"Besides, the most important thing in the world to me is my family. And in order that they may be safe and healthy and happy, I have to stay alive. So I do everything I can to ensure that I do. It is an insecure life and more dangerous that it need be if I don't look after my personal life and my cars to a high level. I know I'm going to have a scratch or a bump from time to time, but I don't wake up at night thinking about accidents. One has to be mature about it."

It took Jackie only a few weeks to get over his Spa accident, bad as it was, and though he missed the French Grand Prix of 1966, he was back for the

While being driven back to Indianapolis from a public appearance in a nearby town in an Indiana State Police car, he helped the trooper catch a car thief and was rewarded with this police billy which he's showing off at the Indy "500" drivers' meeting.

British. Unfortunately, BRM was still using the 2-liter engines, and the Brabhams of Jack Brabham and Denny Hulme were now beginning to dominate races with their 3-liter Repco engines—it was to be Jack's third World Championship year.

Jackie finished fourth in the Dutch GP, fifth in the German, was sidelined in the British (engine) and retired with engine troubles from the last three Grands Prix of the year—in all of which he used the H16. Graham Hill had a pretty depressing year, too, apart from his Indianapolis win, and when Ford offered him a nice sum of money to go back to the Lotus team and run as teammate to Jim Clark, he accepted it. He had spent seven years with BRM, had won the World Driving Championship once, and now felt that he was being regarded "as part of the furniture."

Stewart stayed, and this, too, was a calculated move.

"It was a completely useless year in most ways but I was Number One driver for the first time, and I had certain responsibilities and some rights as a Number One that have served me in good stead during the past two years."

He again went out on the Tasman series to defend his title. Clark's Lotus was the big threat, and the Stewart/Clark battles were indeed something to watch. The two Scots were by now close friends, and their understanding of one another on the track was unsurpassed. On and off the track they both had a lot of fun, but Clark and the Lotus—a type 33, using the same 2-liter Coventry Climax engine for six of the eight races—proved to be vastly superior to anything else in the series, and Jim took the title.

The year's Grand Prix results for Jackie and his BRM read pretty dismally, with one retirement after another, sometimes engine, mostly transmission, with a second place at Spa and a third in the French at Le Mans.

Ferrari had approached Jackie around the time of the Dutch Grand Prix to drive for them in 1968.

"I had to go down there to talk to them because I was in such a bad shape at BRM. I had to look at life fairly and squarely. I was pretty certain I would go to Ferrari, and it was affecting my relationship with BRM—which is the main reason I never like to talk about *next* year until this one is finished. I didn't like doing something behind their backs, and I had to be as honest with them as I could, for their benefit as well as mine. It was at that time that I suggested Len Terry should make a new chassis for the V12, because the chassis for the H16 just wasn't going to do the trick. I went to enormous lengths to persuade Louis Stanley and Tony Rudd. I had to retire very early in the Dutch Grand Prix when the car ran out of brake fluid, so I got on a plane and went back to Scotland that same evening. I wasn't very pleased. Then about two-thirty in the morning Louis Stanley phoned to say he'd got hold of Len Terry, and Len had agreed to make the car.

"I felt very bad about it—there was I talking to Ferrari and there was

BRM going to all that trouble . . . so I told Ferrari I wasn't interested in talking any more until the pitch was cleared."

This dislike Jackie has of "going behind people's backs" is something he shares with Ken Tyrrell, the man who had taught him so much. And when, at the end of 1967, Tyrrell decided to stake everything on running the French Matra chassis with a Ford Cosworth V8 engine in the coming Formula 1 season, Jackie saw the potential, took a calculated risk and joined him.

A Very Near Miss

While Jackie was at BRM, he had been driving in Formula 2 events for Ken Tyrrell. The car they used was a Matra, made by a major French industrial firm dealing mainly in missiles and other space-age equipment. The automotive division is relatively small, and the main commercial product is the Matra Sports car, a 1.7-liter mid-engined two-seater.

The first Matra, a Formula 3 car with an advanced monocoque chassis, was made in 1965. Jean-Pierre Beltoise drove it to its first victory at Reims that year, and results were encouraging enough for Matra to bring out a 2-liter BRM-engined sports car in 1966.

The combination of Tyrrell/Matra/Stewart began in the autumn of 1965, when Ken Tyrrell stood next to the Matra boss at a reception. During the course of a casual conversation it was arranged that Jackie Stewart would carry out some tests in a Formula 2 Matra. As a result, Jackie drove one for Ken during 1966 and 1967.

Both men were impressed by the chassis, and the Ford FVA engine was unbeatable in 1967. Matra intended to produce its own V12 engine for Formula 1 in 1968, but it was obvious to everyone during 1967 that the Cosworth Ford V8 engine was currently by far the best engine for Formula 1,

He won the 1968 Dutch Grand Prix for the first of three Formula 1 victories that year.

and when it became available for sale, Tyrrell was one of Cosworth's first customers.

After a dismal year with BRM, Jackie decided that a new team with a new car might not be such a bad idea, and Ken Tyrrell's Matra Ford setup was named Matra International, with Jackie as the Number 1 driver. The Frenchmen, Jean-Pierre Beltoise, Johnny Servoz-Gavin and Henri Pescarolo, were all to be Matra drivers during the year, sometimes powered by the Matra V12 engine, sometimes by the Ford V8.

The MS9, the car used by Tyrrell and Stewart in the 1968 South African Grand Prix, was a much modified Formula 2 chassis with bigger brakes, 15-inch wheels and a tubular sub-frame around the engine. In the latter part of the 1967 Formula 2 season, Tyrrell's Matras with their Dunlop tires were clearly as good as any of the opposition (mainly Winkelmann Brabhams on Firestones) and the link with Dunlop was strengthened when Jackie and Ken decided to go on using their products in Formula 1. It has been a very fruitful association for all concerned.

The arrangements, then, were as follows. Matra was to supply the cars free of charge while Ken was to buy his own engines at $18,000 each, basically as an insurance against their V12 not being competitive. The team's main sponsors were to be Elf, a French fuel company, and Dunlop. The cars were to be painted French blue, with appropriate decals adding color, and were to be maintained and prepared for races in the Tyrrell workshop (a hut at the far side of his timber yard) at East Horsley in England. The mechanics were mostly British, but Matra loaned the team Bruno Morin, who was to act as liaison between the French firm and this strangely assorted British offshoot. There were other French experts to call on when necessary, and with Ian Mills and Alex Meskell from Dunlop giving an immense amount of technical skill, knowledge and time to the venture, Matra International was off to a good start. They were out to scale the heights of motor racing, nothing less than the top would do, and with all systems apparently "go," they arrived in South Africa.

The car was only finished on Christmas Day, and the race was on January 1st, so it appeared during practice painted in a matt green undercoat. In

After breaking his wrist in early 1968 he was forced to drive with it in a plastic splint. Despite the pain and inconvenience he finished second in the point standings to former teammate Graham Hill.

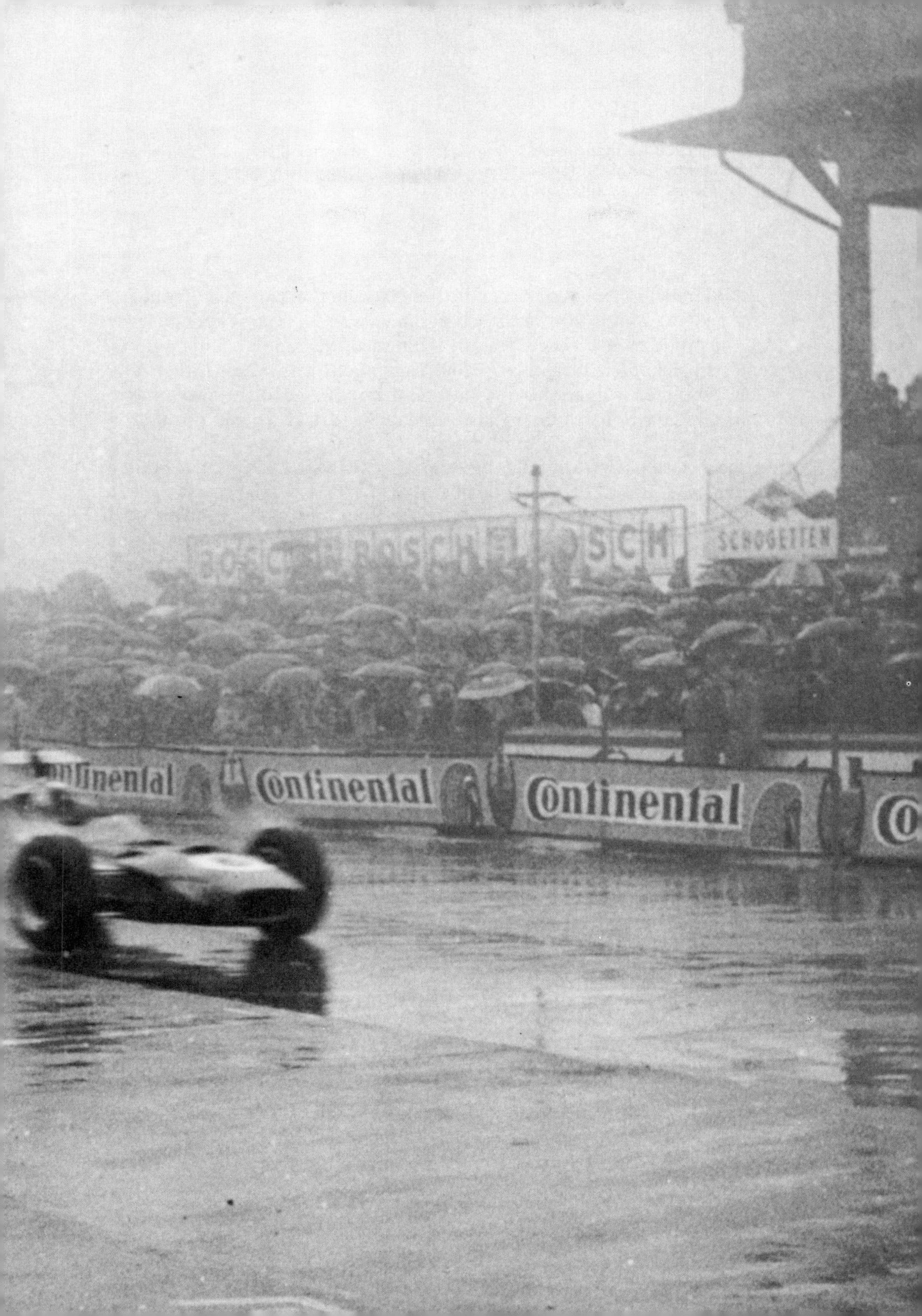
BOSCH
SCHOGETTEN
Continental
Continental
Continental

He won the 1968 German Grand Prix in spite of the fact that heavy rain accompanied by fog made for the worst conditions in more than thirty years. Visibility was as low as fifty yards on some parts of the circuit.

typical Tyrrell fashion, Ken had also brought along a ballasted Formula 2 Matra, and the Matra firm itself had a similar car for Jean-Pierre Beltoise.

On the first day of practice, Stewart astonished everyone by putting up the second best time of 1:24.7—Clark in his Lotus Ford was fastest with 1:23.9. No one else was within two seconds of them. In the other two practice sessions Graham Hill was faster, just pushing Stewart to the end of the front row of the grid by one-tenth of a second.

In the race the Matra led the first lap after Stewart had made a brilliant start, but was passed by Clark on the second. Stewart subsequently had a real battle for second place with Hill, but was put out of the running when his engine put a rod through the side on the forty-fourth lap. Beltoise finished the race, in sixth position, and although Ken's first week's bill for engine repairs was $4000, all concerned were encouraged by the way the new car had shown its paces.

Then came a big setback. At Jarama, Madrid, for a Formula 2 race at the end of April, Jackie crashed at the end of the straight during practice and broke his wrist. Although it was a hairline fracture, he had also damaged a ligament, and the injury was painful and obstinate. It was obvious that he would be out of racing for a few weeks at any rate, and would certainly miss the Spanish Grand Prix and Indianapolis, where he had intended to drive an STP Lotus turbine.

Only three weeks before Jackie's accident, Jimmy Clark had been killed during a Formula 2 race at Hockenheim in Germany. The days after Jimmy's death and the time around the funeral were, Jackie admits, the saddest of his life.

"I was more upset by that than I have ever been over anything. This is part of motor racing I dislike most. We are a closely knit bunch of people and we live very much together. Sometimes I think it is a very futile and meaningless business. . . ."

We all thought rather on those lines as we stood around the crowded,

Although Mario Andretti (following closely behind Stewart) was the fastest qualifier, Jackie led every lap to win the 1968 U.S. Grand Prix.

hushed churchyard at Chirnside, near Jimmy's home in Scotland, on a cold spring day. Virtually the whole of the Grand Prix circus was there, visibly shocked and saddened, wondering what it was all *for,* in the long run. And yet, as Helen said, "Somehow you seem to get hold of yourself and get on." The danger of a fatal accident is an ever-present adjunct to motor racing; we all know it and we've all suffered from it. But it is something we never talk about if we can help it, and something we hate being asked about. This is not an ostrich viewpoint, but there is nothing to be gained from brooding on possible disasters. Jackie has a very common-sense attitude to this.

"One imagines that it never happens to oneself, but at the same time one must be a realist and say that it could happen; so I try to pave the way to making it a slight accident instead of a big one. Sometimes I get a hell of a fright and feel that I would rather be somewhere else at that moment, but I don't stop racing because of it. I go on taking the car to its limits every time, even while I'm tire testing. Every time I drive a racing car I have to take it to nine-tenths—ten-tenths usually means an accident, because then there isn't any margin for even the slightest error."

Jackie can hold forth at length on this subject of the limits to which driver and car can be taken. He sounds remarkably like Stirling Moss on the same subject, and is just as eloquent, just as graphic with his descriptions.

But in May 1968, as he lay out in the sunshine at his new home in Switzerland, waiting for his arm to heal, he must have been feeling that Fate had been unkind. His third bid for the Indy "500," which he had almost won in 1966 and in which he was running third in 1967, when mechanical problems retired him, was now out of the question, and he was not even present when Jean-Pierre Beltoise drove the new Matra MS10 Ford into sixth place in the Spanish Grand Prix at Jarama on May 12th, after leading the race in the early stages. He also missed driving in the Monaco Grand Prix on May 26th, where the V12 Matra made its debut driven by J-P. B., while Johnny Servoz-Gavin was allowed the Matra International entry. Driving with real spirit, Servoz-Gavin acquired a front row position on the grid alongside Graham Hill and made a fantastic start to lead the race for three meteoric laps. Then a drive shaft broke, possibly as a result of Servoz-

The Grand Prix of South Africa, the first Formula 1 race of 1968, saw Matra leading its first GP event. However, Jackie dropped out on the 43rd lap with engine trouble.

Named Matra International and working out of a shop in Tyrrell's timberyard in England, the team consisted of an English owner (Ken), Scottish and French drivers (Stewart and Beltoise) and French cars with English engines.

118

Gavin hitting the chicane on the first lap. Jackie Stewart, with arm in plaster, peered wryly at all this through his sunglasses from the gasworks hairpin and saw Jean-Pierre in the factory Matra hit the chicane and retire with broken suspension, while Graham Hill went on to win for the fourth time on this circuit. With the Spanish and the Monaco GPs under his belt, Graham was clearly the man to beat when Jackie resumed operations.

This he did at Spa, for the Belgian GP. Jackie's arm was still in plaster, and his doctors would have liked him to rest it completely for a good deal longer. Jackie used the same MS10 chassis which Johnny Servoz-Gavin had driven with such verve at Monaco. It was a pretty extraordinary race, with eight cars finishing out of a field of eighteen. Chris Amon achieved the pole position, with Jackie alongside him. Chris led on the first lap, with Surtees in the Honda overtaking him on the second and leading for nine laps. Amon got a stone through the radiator of his Ferrari and retired, then Surtees dropped out with a suspension failure, which left Hulme in the lead from Stewart. There was a good battle between these two for seven laps, until Hulme went out with a broken drive shaft, and Jackie was leading the race.

For fifteen arduous laps of this long, fast circuit he was way out in front, till his lead was twenty-five seconds over McLaren. We were all waiting, pencils poised, to tick off his penultimate lap, and preparing to celebrate his tremendous achievement, when the blue car, instead of flashing past, came roaring into the pits—it had run out of fuel! If that had been all, he could probably still have won the race, but when he had refueled he tried to restart the car, and couldn't. The battery was flat. It took four minutes to change it, and during this time Bruce McLaren's orange car had gone by into the lead, closely followed by Pedro Rodriguez in a BRM. Although his mechanic held out a board to show his changed fortunes, Bruce apparently did not see it, and was the most surprised winner I've seen in many a year.

Stewart charged onto the track again while the checkered flag was being held out, and completed another lap to finish fourth, but it was a crying disappointment. He had driven beautifully, with his right wrist stiff and sore, and it would have been a truly runaway win.

Two weeks later Jackie won the Dutch Grand Prix at Zandvoort in drenching and virtually non-stop rain. The visibility was so bad I abandoned my lap chart at about quarter distance and retired, in tears, to a Dutch friend's car to drink coffee and feel a real failure! Meanwhile, Jackie, driving with his arm laced into a plastic support, finished over a minute and a half ahead of Jean-Pierre Beltoise's V12 Matra. His car was running on Dunlop's all-purpose tires with a circumferential drainage groove. The conditions were so bad that Hill, McLaren, Brabham and Courage all went off the road, and Beltoise had a monumental spin into the sand at the side of the track. But Jackie won mainly because of his smooth driving, and great was the jubilation in the Dunlop caravan after the race, where champagne was flowing freely.

The French Grand Prix was an appalling race which everyone would rather forget, including Jackie Ickx, whose first Grand Prix victory it was. The Rouen circuit could be described as a miniature Spa; it has many potentially dangerous sections, for the spectators and marshals as well as the drivers. The organization of this race was particularly amateurish and riddled with politics—there was very little practice time; the first session started late and finished early because the noise was interfering with the local TV station and General de Gaulle was due to give a speech! The total practice time over the two days was woefully inadequate, particularly for people trying to learn the circuit.

It was at this time, too, that wings and spoilers began to be taken seriously, and grew, and grew . . . Jackie Oliver learned the effects of aerodynamic disturbance the hard way, as he came out of another driver's slipstream and promptly careered off the road, demolishing his Lotus against a wall.

It was raining fairly hard at the start of the race, which was late, and very soon it was pouring down. On the second lap Jo Schlesser's Honda hit a grassy bank, crashed back onto the track and became a fiery inferno. Most of the other drivers crept by the wreckage and continued, but Schlesser died and the whole event was spoiled. Ickx's well-deserved victory in a Ferrari was overshadowed by it. Stewart finished third.

"I didn't drive well in Rouen," says Jackie, "I was driving badly, the tires weren't all that super—but they were the same I used at Zandvoort. No, I just wasn't in the picture that day. My coordination was wrong and I was nervous—it wasn't wrist trouble, it was me. The car and I weren't getting on that day."

The British GP was held at Brands Hatch, which is a very twisty circuit with a lot of gear changes and involves much use of the wrists. Jackie suffered more pain during that race than in any other season, and he couldn't do any better than sixth, while Jo Siffert won *his* first Grand Prix.

Jackie describes the German GP himself.

"The conditions were foul, but I think I drove quite well. We had an advantage on tires, I'm sure of that. The visibility was so poor we were

Pointing to the plaster cast on his wrist, Jackie explains why he'll be unable to drive in either the Spanish Grand Prix or the Indianapolis "500."

120

driving by instinct. I am a very slow learner in a lot of things, but on a circuit, once I have got a thing established in my mind, it doesn't often go away, and I think it was one of the occasions when this was of enormous value."

He won the German. Pictures of the race show what looks at first like a series of fast boats throwing up big bow waves. There was also thick fog. It was a masterly piece of driving, and put Jackie second in the Championship point standings behind Graham Hill, with twenty-six points to thirty.

At Monza there was a good battle between Stewart and Hulme, with Siffert mixing it with them whenever possible. Denny went on to win when Jackie's engine failed on lap forty-eight. Now both Hulme and Ickx were challenging Hill and Stewart for the Championship, and the last three races, the transatlantic ones, were vital.

Hulme won again in Canada, at St. Jovite. Every car in the race now had some sort of wing, and the start pictures looked more like the take-off for an air race than a motor race. It was here that Jackie Ickx's bid for the Championship ended when his Ferrari's throttle stuck open during practice and he crashed, breaking a leg. Stewart finished sixth after a ten-minute pit stop for a suspension repair.

Watkins Glen was Jackie's race—although it had seemed it might be Andretti's at first. But there was only .07 of a second between them as they lined up on the front row of the starting grid. After Andretti's front air foil had broken, and he'd lost time in the pits, Stewart pulled away until he was forty seconds in the lead. David Phipps describes his performance like this.

"Stewart's victory was his third of the year. His driving was a model of consistency—he built up a good lead and then eased off slightly, just as Jim Clark used to—and the whole Tyrrell Organisation functioned as a racing team should."

Jackie's thoughts were on the same lines. "I enjoyed Watkins Glen. I thought of Jimmy, because it was a race that he would have won—you know, he won his races like this: he got an early start and he took advantage of it and he didn't let anyone get near thereafter. He controlled the pace, and when I was winning that race I thought of him a lot. I got a lot of pleasure out of feeling that I had done the job the way it should be done."

Now everything hinged on the last race of the season, the Mexican Grand Prix. The Championship points table showed Graham Hill at the top with

Three drivers had a chance to become World Driving Champion of 1968 in the final race of the year, the Mexican Grand Prix. Denis Hulme was eliminated when he crashed (without injury). Graham Hill, in the lead here, and Jackie, trying to come through on the inside, staged a battle royal for the lead until the halfway point when Stewart's engine began to go sour.

thirty-nine, Jackie second with thirty-seven and Denny Hulme third with thirty-four. Any one of the three could be World Driving Champion.

The practice sessions were jittery and trouble-filled, and it was Jo Siffert who dominated proceedings and secured the pole position. Hill and Hulme were on the second row, behind Amon and Siffert, and Stewart was in the fourth row. He had broken a drive shaft yoke in the last practice session, puncturing his tire and wrecking the suspension and the wing. He took over the second car from Servoz-Gavin and got down to a time that would put him on the third row. But he didn't want to race that car, because it had been involved in a fire in the garage at Watkins Glen, so he opted for the other, which had to be rebuilt. It was not a happy day.

The Tyrrell mechanics did a wonderful job to get the car ready for the race, but Jackie had no time to try it first.

The race began with all kinds of "ifs" and "buts." Hill had to keep Stewart behind him to be Champion. Jackie had to finish first, if Graham were allowed to be second. Hulme had to knock both of them out, somehow. But Hulme's chances vanished when a rear damper broke as he came onto the pit straight. The car smashed into the guard rail opposite the pits, wrecked the suspension and started a small fire. Denny was all right, but the car was immediately inundated with foam, marshals, police and officialdom.

Now it was between Jackie and Graham, and it was a battle royal. Until the thirty-eighth lap there was not much in it; first one would do a fast lap, then the other, never more than two or three seconds between them, with Hill in front. Then the gap suddenly widened to five seconds, then fifteen—the Matra's engine wasn't getting enough fuel to run above 6500 rpm, and Jackie couldn't do anything about it. He finished seventh. Graham Hill was World Driving Champion.

The long and the short of a winning team.

Achievement

The Stewart/Matra/Tyrrell/Dunlop group moved into 1969 with a single-minded determination to take the title that had so narrowly escaped them the year before. Everyone connected with the effort went about his own job in a very professional way, with no half measures tolerated.

The secret of Ken Tyrrell's success is very thorough preparation. Nothing is left to chance. The spare car is always in the pits, full of fuel, just in case anything goes wrong on the warm-up lap. And during practice, however short, both cars are run with full tanks to make sure they will behave properly in the early part of the race. Ken gives the credit for these habits to Jackie— "he suggests things and we follow them up"—but it is largely the solid, trust-inspiring, dependable character of Ken Tyrrell that keeps the team running smoothly.

The Matra itself, the MS80 which Stewart used for the major part of the year, is not particularly revolutionary, but it holds together. It has very good traction and is one of the strongest cars in motor racing. In the era of suspension-mounted wings, Matra was one of the few teams which never had any breakages. When in doubt, the Matra designers always err on the heavy side—the opposite philosophy from that of Lotus.

After winning the 1969 Dutch Grand Prix, Jackie said it was one of the most tiring he had ever driven.

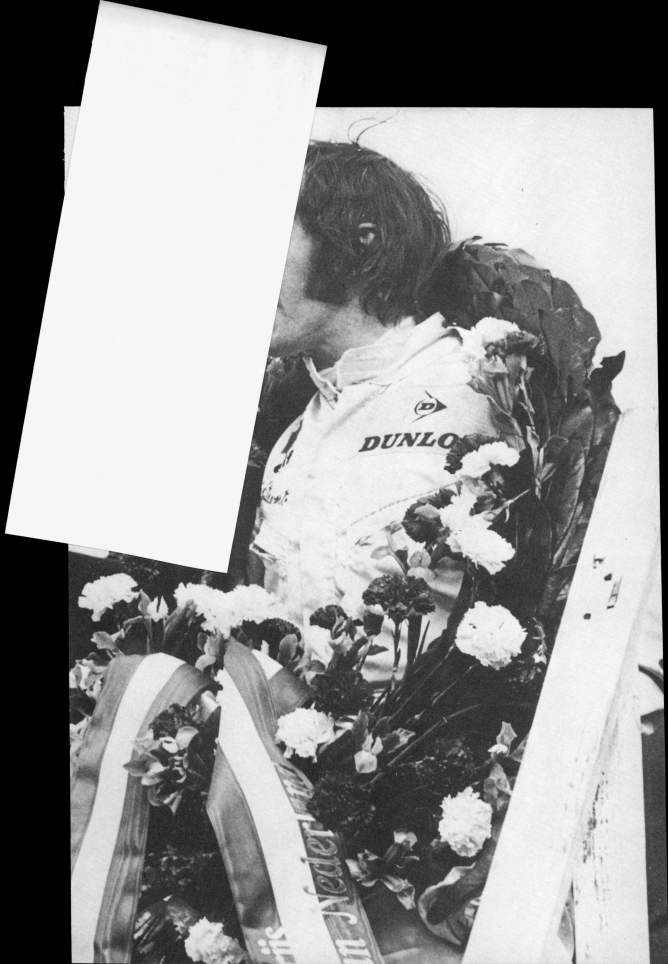

FERODO

Shell

Dunlop put a lot of money, time and research into their '68-'69 tires, and Jackie has repaid them in full with his fierce loyalty, his many public appearances and his success. The Dunlop rain tires undoubtedly helped Jackie to dominate the saturated races of 1968, and though now it appears that Goodyear has come up with some winners—they scored two victories in the last three races of 1969—it is certain that Jackie will stay with Dunlop and that they will spare nothing to give him tires fit for a Champion.

As for Jackie, he is undoubtedly the sort of driver of whom every team manager dreams. Of all the drivers in Grand Prix racing today, Stewart is one of the easiest on his equipment. He normally shifts gears well below the rev limit, and tries to avoid doing anything sudden or violent. His style is deceptively smooth. The Matra was very twitchy over some circuits this year, but Jackie usually made it look easy. He never rushes into a situation wildly, and hasn't much good to say about those drivers who do. He doesn't really enjoy racing at close quarters, particularly with people he can't rely on; but if it is necessary, as at Monza, to join in a slipstreaming battle, he will do it in the same calm, calculated way as any other form of driving.

Ken Tyrrell says he is incredibly sensitive to the car and whatever might be wrong with it. Although Jackie is a fully trained mechanic himself, he never interferes with Tyrrell's organization, or tries to wield a spanner every time he comes into the pits. He says his apprenticeship and the knowledge of tuning and preparation he gained in Scotland are useful when it comes to diagnosing trouble, but he has great confidence in Ken and his mechanics.

Jackie also has the invaluable gift of self-control. He keeps himself totally in hand, not by clamming-up and hiding in a transporter before a race, as some drivers need to do, but laughing and talking his way out of irritations in such a natural way that no one would guess the pressures he is enduring inwardly. I have heard him swear—often—seen him recoil from some particularly annoying pursuer, but he keeps his temper and remembers his manners under great provocation.

It seemed as if nothing could stop the string of Stewart victories in 1969. After wrecking his car in practice, Jackie took over the car of his teammate Beltoise and won the British Grand Prix. He then had five victories out of six races.

With all these natural gifts, plus a good car and a good team, Jackie began his assault on the 1969 Championship.

He started the year well by winning the South African Grand Prix on March 1st. There was a new car now, the Matra MS80, but Jackie decided to stick with the well-tried MS10 for this race. It now sported twin airfoils for the first time, like the Brabhams, while Lotus had two tall airfoils *and* a pair of front "fins." Wings were gradually getting overemphasized, and failures were numerous.

Brabham gained the pole position with Rindt and Hulme alongside him, while Stewart was with Amon on the second row. But as the first six cars were all credited with times between 1:20 and 1:20.8, it was obviously anyone's race.

Somehow, Jackie shot into the lead from the second row right at the start, and stayed in front till the checkered flag fell at the end of eighty laps. Jochen Rindt, in his first drive for Team Lotus, had engine trouble; Brabham lost his wing, which caused his engine to overrev on the straight, and Hulme ran a good race to finish in third place, behind Hill. Neither of these drivers was ever any dire threat to Stewart, who won by 18.8 seconds after easing off considerably during the last few laps.

Two weeks later Jackie ran the MS80 at Brands Hatch in the Race of the Champions. This was, in fact, the first real Formula 1 Matra, as distinct from the previous scaled-up Formula 2 cars, and it was an immediate success, as Jackie won the race by again leading from start to finish. Graham Hill had been on the pole, and Jo Siffert had recorded the same time as Jackie, but the Matra shot away to build up an early, demoralizing lead, and we all went to Barcelona two weeks later expecting a Stewart walkover.

But in practice for the Spanish Grand Prix we saw some surprises. Chris Amon, in his Ferrari, was very fast on the first day, and the Lotuses of Hill and Rindt with their gigantic wings and enlarged front fins began to show very good results on the second day, while Jackie's engine seemed to be suffering from some form of fuel starvation. On the third day of practice on

The MS80 was the first real Formula 1 Matra, the others Jackie had been driving were merely scaled-up Formula 2 cars. The new car proved an immediate success as Stewart led the 1969 Race of Champions from start to finish.

132

this beautiful, twisty circuit around a hilly park in Barcelona, Colin Chapman went just one step too far with the wings, taping pieces of aluminum along the back of the rear ones. This had the effect of adding such immense downward thrust on the rear wheels that the roadholding was vastly improved. Rindt brought his lap time down by a full second to 1:25.2, Amon remained on the front row with 1:26.2 and Graham pushed Jackie into the second row with 1:26.6.

The two factory Lotuses, Siffert's Lotus and Amon's Ferrari streaked off the line at the start, and before the first corner Rindt had a lead of about three car lengths. Stewart was sixth, then overtook Brabham for fifth place, and then all the drama began. Hill's airfoil failed and he shot off into a guard rail on the left of the track, spun wildly across to hit the guard rail on the right and demolished his car, luckily without injury to himself or anyone else. Soon afterwards it could be seen that Rindt's car, far away in the lead, was about to lose a wing, too, but before anyone could do anything to warn him, his car went out of control at the same place as Graham's, struck the barrier, leaped into the air, turned over and landed upside down on top of Jochen. He was very, very lucky to escape with minor facial injuries.

Now Amon was left to take over Rindt's first place, and when Siffert retired with engine trouble Amon had a forty-second lead over Stewart, whose engine, though changed overnight, was no better than the first one and wouldn't pick up properly. Amon's engine, however, blew up just after the pits on lap fifty-seven, and now it was just a question of whether Stewart would survive this punishing race. Ickx was his only threat, and when the young Belgian had the wing of his Brabham collapse, that was the end of the challenge. Stewart won the Spanish Grand Prix, the first of the five finishers. He calls it a lucky win, because his car was certainly not truly competitive that day, but at least the wings stayed on!

At Monaco, a fortnight later, wings were banned. The danger from flying metal and the sudden loss of traction caused by their failure prompted a lot

133

Trying to pass Stewart on the way into a fast downhill left-hander during the 1969 Canadian Grand Prix proved to be an error in judgment on the part of Jackie Ickx whose Brabham collided with Stewart's Matra and caused it to spin off the track while they were dueling for the lead.

After battling Jochen Rindt for the lead during the first third of the United States Grand Prix, Jackie was forced out with engine trouble.

of anti-wing publicity, and Jochen Rindt's statements regarding the Barcelona incident hastened their demise. The organizers said, "No wings," after the first practice session, and there was quite a furore in the Principality that evening. Stewart had covered the Monte Carlo circuit faster than anyone ever before, ending the day with a 1:24.9, and Tyrrell was understandably put out when the ban was announced. As he and other team managers and constructors pointed out, the cars were made and set up on the principle that wings would be an intrinsic part, and removing them would be dangerous too. The ban, however, was kept, and early next morning the cars appeared looking very naked and odd. Wings had been with us for almost a year, and we had grown used to them—almost fond of them. No one expected to see times below 1:26 (Thursday's times were declared null and void), but Jackie still managed to lap in 1:25.6, with Hill only one fifth of a second slower.

The last practice session on Saturday proved conclusively that Stewart could fly with or without wings, when he claimed the pole position with 1:24.6. Amon was next at 1:25.

Stewart led away from the line, and soon pulled out a handsome lead, while behind him the usual game of ten-little-Indian-boys was being played, Oliver, Brabham, Surtees, Rodriguez, Moser and Amon dropping out before the twentieth lap. Stewart was twenty-six seconds in front of Hill when he stopped at the chicane on lap twenty-three with a broken universal joint. Graham went on to win Monaco for the fifth time, and closed to within three points of Stewart in the World Championship.

At Zandvoort in the Dutch Grand Prix, the front row was Rindt, Stewart, Hill. The weather was bright and dry, and Rindt was really fast. Everyone had some sort of modified wing to meet the new requirements of motor racing's governing body, the Commission Sportive Internationale. Matra and Lotus both produced their four-wheel-drive cars for the first time, but neither was fast enough nor reliable enough to race.

Rindt pulled out an enormous lead in the early laps, exactly as he had at Barcelona, but on the sixteenth lap there was a whirring noise just as he went

During the early stages of the Grand Prix of Monaco, Stewart and Chris Amon (right behind) were pulling away from everyone else in the field. Though obviously the fastest, neither of these two finished the race.

Jackie apparently had a premonition that he would sew up the Championship at the Italian Grand Prix, for although he never brings the children to races, the entire family showed up at Monza.

Stewart considers his win at the 1969 Spanish Grand Prix as being lucky, for many cars were faster than his that day, but he managed to be the first of only five cars that finished the race.

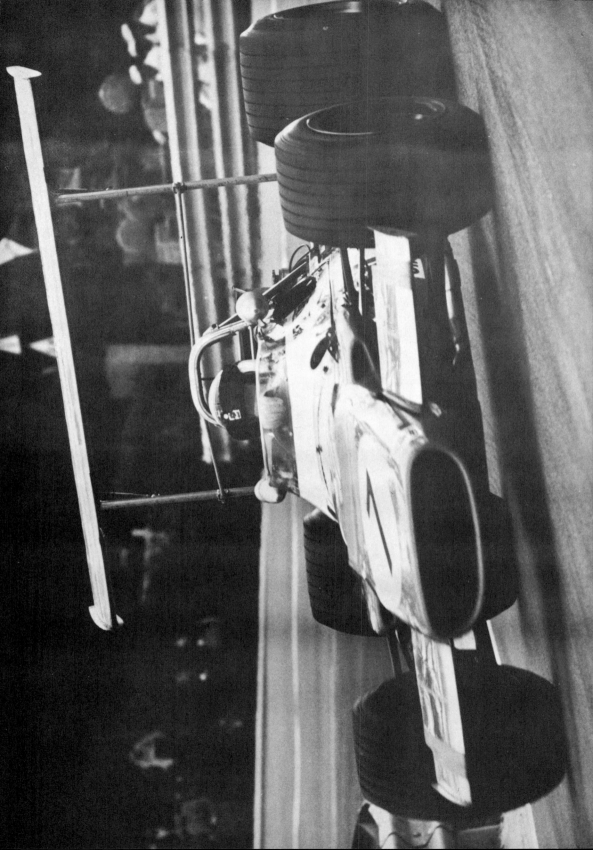

past the pits. Another Lotus drive shaft had broken. Stewart now had a good lead from Siffert, and his car gave him no trouble. He never put a foot wrong all through the race, but he regards it as one of the most tiring he's ever driven. He had now notched up three wins out of four GPs, and had a twelve-point lead over Hill.

And so we all moved on to Clermont-Ferrand for the French Grand Prix and watched the French cars come in first and second, Beltoise just passing Ickx for second place on the last lap before a wildly jubilant, patriotic crowd. Jackie dominated the whole meeting, being fastest in each practice session, leading from start to finish and lapping everyone in the race except Beltoise and Ickx. Hill's car wouldn't handle properly, and Rindt was forced to retire because of nausea created by the twisty, switchback circuit. Hulme lay second until an anti-roll bar upright broke. But no one else was remotely in the running.

It seemed altogether too much to expect this run of victories to continue, and during the last practice for the British Grand Prix, at Silverstone, Stewart had one of his rare "moments." Coming round Woodcote, the fast corner before the pits, he hit a piece of concrete curbing which had been dislodged by hot weather and a lot of other people's wheels. A rear tire burst and the Matra spun across the track into a grass bank. Without wasting a moment, Jackie leaped out, flagged the other drivers down as they came into sight, then ran across and took over Beltoise's car to finish off the day's training with only a fractional reduction in speed.

In spite of the accident, Jackie was on the front row between Rindt and Hulme. The latter retired with a broken camshaft, while Jochen and Jackie had a heart-stopping tussle for the lead which Jochen looked as if he might retain till the end. But the meeting was a disastrous one for Lotus. One of the end plates of the airfoil on Jochen's car started to come adrift and foul the tire. A pit stop to tear it off lost him first place, but the final humiliation came when all three Lotuses ran out of fuel during the last laps—first Rindt, then Hill, then Siffert.

An obviously elated Helen joins Jackie in Victory Circle at Monza.

Once again it was Stewart who received the victor's laurels, and he was already in an almost unassailable position in the Championship.

When Jackie Ickx won the German Grand Prix, beating Stewart into second place, one would have thought by the gloomy faces of Jackie and Ken and the Dunlop people that the sky had fallen! Stewart led initially, but Ickx, who had made a bad start, worked his way up to second place in three laps of the fourteen-mile circuit. For the next three laps the Matra and the Brabham were only a few yards apart, but then Stewart began to have gearshift trouble and Ickx took over the lead. He drove beautifully, proved himself a master of the difficult Nürburgring, and he deserved to win—though it would have been a very close thing but for Jackie's problems.

Having failed to clinch the Championship in Germany, Jackie and Ken had no intention of letting it slip any farther away from them in Italy. As if to announce his intentions, Jackie brought along his two sons to the Monza circuit, something of which neither he nor Helen really approve; but with his unerring judgment of the right *time* for various actions, Jackie anticipated that photographers would be wanting some family pictures if he should now take the Champion's crown from Graham Hill. And anyway, the Villa d'Este on Lake Como, where they were all staying, is a paradise too good for one's children to miss.

What a fantastic race that was! Monza is a unique circuit and not quite fair on drivers or machinery. All the time you keep up in somebody's slipstream everything is fine. Lose your tow and you drop back. Practice this year developed into a sort of game, with bunches of cars circulating together, taking advantage of faster cars for a tow and then coming out of the slipstream at the appropriate moment and hurtling past the timekeepers.

Jochen Rindt secured the pole position partly because he joined in a friendly, pre-arranged slipstreaming session with Piers Courage; several other drivers put up fast times in the same way. But Jackie, being the driver they were all out to beat, did his best time—third fastest—all on his own, and it put him on the second row of the two-by-two grid.

It looked as if it would be another Rindt/Stewart race, with Denny Hulme all keen to make Monza the scene of a victory such as he had enjoyed the year before. In the event it was Rindt, Stewart, Courage, Siffert, Hill, Hulme, Beltoise and McLaren who slogged it out together, with the final four contenders coming around almost in a straight line across the track on the last lap—Stewart, Rindt, Beltoise and McLaren. It was more like the end of a horse race, with the judges calling for a photo-finish decision. But it was Stewart's race by about half a car length, with Beltoise and McLaren a few feet behind. Jackie Stewart was now, without any doubt at all, World Champion racing driver of 1969.

After that high point, the three transatlantic races were a bit of a let-down. In the Canadian it was a Stewart/Ickx duel, with Rindt left far behind, which ended when Jackie Ickx tried to pass Stewart in an awkward—not to say dangerous—place, touched his rear wheel and spun him off the track. Jackie couldn't restart his Matra, so he walked back to the pits with a grimmer face than is usual for this ebullient young man.

Stewart put in a great many practice laps for the U.S. Grand Prix, a lot of them with the four-wheel-drive Matra, but he was once again on the second row in the MS80 with Rindt and Hulme in front of him. Denny, however, had the misfortune to have his gearshift linkage break before the start, and he subsequently lost twenty-one laps having it replaced.

So the old pattern repeated itself again—Stewart and Rindt out at the front, and then the three Brabhams of Courage, Ickx and Brabham fighting it out in the next group. (Hill's car never seemed to go fast enough in this race, and later a tire came off its rim causing him to crash. The leg injuries he suffered kept him out of racing for several months.)

Jackie managed to pass Rindt, but never got away from him, and soon Jochen reclaimed the lead. At first Jackie managed to keep up with him, but then his engine began to sound rough, and he dropped back more and more, finally retiring to the pits on lap thirty-six. Jochen went on to win his first Grand Prix, a reward he had long deserved. He has been Stewart's chief rival throughout the year, and most likely will continue to be in 1970.

Mexico was Denny Hulme's race, at last; he had had many front row starts and yet had not had a trouble-free race since Zandvoort. The Mexican GP was really more of a tire war than anything, with Goodyear's G20s proving much superior to the opposition. Stewart won the "non-Goodyear" race, finishing fourth behind Hulme, Ickx and Brabham.

Denny and Jackie shared the winner's champagne, for only now could it be officially stated that Jackie was World Driving Champion. The season was over.

And what of 1970? Matra has refused to sell Tyrrell chassis for the

coming year, and intend running an all-French team. Jackie insists upon staying with Tyrrell, Ford and Dunlop, and has settled to drive a car that has not yet been seen—a Formula 1 March. This is an entirely new venture involving designer Robin Herd, who was mainly responsible for the McLaren and the Cosworth F/1 cars, plus some excellent managers who have drummed up a vast amount of sponsorship in a few months. Whether this car will be a suitable vehicle for a World Champion remains to be seen, but as so much hangs on it I expect everything possible will be done to see that it is truly competitive in 1970. March intends to run a factory team as well, and has simply agreed to sell chassis to the Tyrrell organization. The engine will be the V8 Cosworth Ford, which still has plenty of potential.

One of the questions Jackie is asked most often is what he would do if he were to retire from racing—and this he would only do if forced by circumstances or if he suddenly found he disliked it, which is what happened with his clay-pigeon shooting.

"To stop being a racing driver when one is still enjoying it would be a big task—an enormous transformation. I think I would like to get into some sort of financial management. I enjoy the idea of investment, because of my connections with various people in Switzerland whom I see working at that kind of thing and doing a very interesting job. I think if I did that along with some form of promotion, such as the type of work the McCormack organization does, I would have my hands full. That appeals to me.

"When you are a professional racing driver you cannot have a second string. Right now I am making more money out of my racing than I could ever do in organizing anything else. Any business that makes more than, say, £10,000 a year for its principal director is a good business. I can make more than that just making appearances, and advertising the odd product—a lot more. Things such as being at a hill climb in Austria doing a P.R. job for the organizers, or my Rolex watch contract. I wear a Rolex watch anyway, this is simply cashing in on the fact, for them and for me.

"Now, if I can get people to manage my affairs to keep me fully occupied while I am not racing—things like personal appearances, endorsing products—I can make more money than in fooling around with some business I can't give my full time to. I would half do the job and then run off for a motor race, which is not sensible at all."

Because he believes in this attitude very strongly, Jackie puts his heart and soul into whatever he is doing, whether racing, or making speeches, or presenting trophies, or making television appearances. But when he relaxes he does that wholeheartedly too. When he *is* at home, which is not very often now that he has taken on the role of World Champion with such dedication, a typical day goes like this.

"Generally I waken at about eight or eight-thirty and see the children getting up and having their breakfast. I go down and get the mail and take it back to bed. I sit in bed and read my mail, make some phone calls, and I might even go back to sleep. I get up about ten or ten-thirty, have a shower and come down and lie out in the sun till the boys have lunch about twelve. I just lie on a Li-Lo and read—books like *Airport,* or anything by Alastair MacLean, or good adventure books—then I have my lunch about one and have a snooze afterwards while the boys have their nap. When they get up again around two-thirty, I usually play with them for a while, and when Paul gets his tea and bath about five I go down to his playroom and make Lego trains or cars or read to him. He goes to bed at six and I come up to read the English daily papers, which the Nanny fetches in the afternoon. Then I usually take another shower, and have dinner.

"I tend to want to eat at home when we are here, because I literally live in restaurants when I'm away. I don't see very much of Switzerland as a place—I haven't even seen the bottom of my own garden! I haven't been down in the wood yet. Sometimes I go up to the top of the hill on the other side of the road. That is our land as well; in all about six and a half acres. I've never been on the Lake in a steamer. Nor up to the Glaciers. I keep saying we should but we never do, because when I get home I think it is fabulous and I stay home. I like to play golf. But I'm not allowed to snow-ski—my contract stipulates that I shouldn't in case I break something. However, I have rented a chalet at Villars for the winter and I'm going to see that Helen and the boys learn to ski. They are going to live in Switzerland, and they have to be bilingual, and they have to be able to ski. I like living here. We all do."

Jackie Stewart calls himself "a hungry driver." He wants the best that life can offer, and it really seems that the boy who left school at fifteen to be "a garage man" has got most of the best things in life just now. But he hopes that his two sons will not take up racing.

"I would be terribly worried every day of the year. I certainly wouldn't encourage them. One racing driver in the family is quite enough!"

But why does he drive if, as he admits, he thinks of it as basically a selfish and dangerous sport?

"First and foremost because I enjoy driving. Here I am, a young man of thirty getting large sums of money to do something he would almost want to *pay* to do. It is a very happy situation. And I think I have been darned lucky!"

For 1970 the car was a new creation—a March—that had never been raced. However, the Stewart/Tyrrell touch was there and the car won the Spanish Grand Prix which was only its second race.

Just for the Record

Jackie Stewart's
Formula 1 Races

1964

Dec. 12	Rand GP, Kyalami (ZA)	Lotus Climax 33	Heat 1: R—broken drive shaft Heat 2: 1st

1965

Jan. 1	South African GP, East London	BRM P261	6th
Mar. 13	Race of Champions, Brands Hatch (GB)	BRM P261	Heat 1: 7th Heat 2: 4th Overall result: 2nd
Apr. 12	Sunday Mirror Trophy, Goodwood (GB)	BRM P261	R—engine
May 15	Daily Express Trophy, Silverstone (GB)	BRM P261	1st
May 30	Monaco GP, Monte Carlo	BRM P261	3rd
June 13	European GP, Spa-Francorchamps (B)	BRM P261	2nd
June 27	French GP, Clermont-Ferrand	BRM P261	2nd
July 10	British GP, Silverstone	BRM P261	5th
July 18	Dutch GP, Zandvoort	BRM P261	2nd
Aug. 1	German GP, Nürburgring	BRM P261	R—suspension
Sept. 12	Italian GP, Monza	BRM P261	1st
Oct. 3	United States GP, Watkins Glen	BRM P261	R—suspension

Oct. 24	Mexican GP, Mexico City	BRM P261	R—clutch

1966

May 22	Monaco GP, Monte Carlo	BRM P261	1st
June 12	Belgian GP, Spa-Francorchamps	BRM P261	R—accident
July 16	British GP, Brands Hatch	BRM P261	R—engine
July 24	Dutch GP, Zandvoort	BRM P261	4th
Aug. 7	German GP, Nürburgring	BRM P261	5th
Sept. 4	Italian GP, Monza	BRM P83	R—fuel leak
Sept. 17	Gold Cup, Oulton Park (GB)	BRM P83	R—engine
Oct. 2	United States GP, Watkins Glen	BRM P83	R—engine
Oct. 23	Mexican GP, Mexico City	BRM P83	R—oil leak

1967

Jan. 2	South African GP, Kyalami	BRM P83	R—engine
Apr. 15	Spring Cup, Oulton Park (GB)	BRM P83	Heat 1: R—Fuel pump belt Heat 2: 4th Final: R—suspension
Apr. 29	Daily Express Trophy, Silverstone (GB)	BRM P83	R—transmission
May 7	Monaco GP, Monte Carlo	BRM P261	R—transmission
June 4	Dutch GP, Zandvoort	BRM P83	R—brakes

June 18	Belgian GP, Spa-Francorchamps	BRM P83	2nd
July 2	French GP, Bugatti au Mans	BRM P261	3rd
July 15	British GP, Silverstone	BRM P83	R—transmission
Aug. 6	German GP, Nürburgring	BRM P115	R—transmission
Aug. 27	Canadian GP, Mosport	BRM P115	R—sand in throttle slides
Sept. 10	European GP, Monza (I)	BRM P115	R—engine
Oct. 1	United States GP, Watkins Glen	BRM P115	R—Fuel injection drive belt
Oct. 22	Mexican GP, Mexico City	BRM P115	R—vibration
Nov. 11	Spanish GP, Jarama	Matra Ford MS7	R—accident

1968

Jan. 1	South African GP, Kyalami	Matra Ford MS9	R—engine
Mar. 17	Race of Champions, Brands Hatch (GB)	Matra Ford MS10	6th
June 9	Belgian GP, Spa-Francorchamps	Matra Ford MS10	4th
June 23	Dutch GP, Zandvoort	Matra Ford MS10	1st
July 7	French GP, Rouen	Matra Ford MS10	3rd
July 20	British GP, Brands Hatch	Matra Ford MS10	6th
Aug. 4	European GP, Nürburgring (D)	Matra Ford MS10	1st
Aug. 17	Guards Gold Cup, Oulton Park (GB)	Matra Ford MS10	1st
Sept. 8	Italian GP, Monza	Matra Ford MS10	R—engine

154

Sept. 22	Canadian GP, St. Jovite	Matra Ford MS10 6th
Oct. 6	United States GP, Watkins Glen	Matra Ford MS10 1st
Nov. 3	Mexican GP, Mexico City	Matra Ford MS10 7th

1969

Mar. 1	South African GP, Kyalami	Matra Ford MS10 1st
Mar. 16	Race of Champions, Brands Hatch (GB)	Matra Ford MS80 1st
Mar. 30	Daily Express Trophy, Silverstone (GB)	Matra Ford MS10 3rd
May 4	Spanish GP, Montjuich Park	Matra Ford MS80 1st
June 8	Monaco GP, Monte Carlo	Matra Ford MS80 R—drive shaft
June 21	Dutch GP, Zandvoort	Matra Ford MS80 1st
July 6	French GP, Clermont-Ferrand	Matra Ford MS80 1st
July 19	British GP, Silverstone	Matra Ford MS80 1st
Aug. 3	German GP, Nürburgring	Matra Ford MS80 2nd
Aug. 16	Guards Gold Cup, Oulton Park (GB)	Matra Ford MS80 9th
Sept. 8	Italian GP, Monza	Matra Ford MS80 1st
Sept. 20	Canadian GP, Mosport	Matra Ford MS80 R—accident
Oct. 5	United States GP, Watkins Glen	Matra Ford MS80 R—engine
Oct. 19	Mexican GP, Mexico City	Matra Ford MS80 4th

Jackie Stewart's
Motor Racing Victories

1961				**mph**
Sept. 24	GT over 1600cc	Aston Martin DB4GT	Charterhall, GB	77.50
1962				
Apr. 29	Sports 1600cc	Marcos Ford GT	Charterhall, GB	76.17
Oct. 7	Sports over 1600cc	Jaguar E-type	Charterhall, GB	—
Oct. 7	GT cars	Jaguar E-type	Charterhall, GB	80.80
1963				
Apr. 13	GT cars	Jaguar E-type	Rufforth, GB	63.68
Apr. 13	Sports & GT Cars	Jaguar E-type	Rufforth, GB	63.97
Apr. 28	Sports cars	Jaguar E-type	Charterhall, GB	75.90
June 23	GT cars	Jaguar E-type	Ouston, GB	—
June 30	GT over 1300cc	Tojeiro Buick EE	Charterhall, GB	82.63
Aug. 5	Sports cars	Cooper Climax Monaco T49	Snetterton, GB	94.83
Aug. 5	GT cars	Tojeiro Buick EE	Snetterton, GB	92.35
Aug. 31	Formule Libre	Cooper Climax Monaco T49	Oulton Park, GB	89.97
Aug. 31	Sports cars	Cooper Climax Monaco T49	Oulton Park, GB	91.67
Sept. 21	Formule Libre	Cooper Climax Monaco T49	Goodwood, GB	96.88
Sept. 21	GT over 1150cc	Tojeiro Buick EE	Goodwood, GB	94.06
Sept. 28	Five-hour relay race	Jaguar E-type	Oulton Park, GB	81.60
Sept. 29	Racing Cars	Cooper Climax Monaco T49	Charterhall, GB	89.83
Sept. 29	Sports over 1300cc	Cooper Climax Monaco T49	Charterhall, GB	89.60

156

1964

Mar. 14	Formula 3	Cooper BMC T72	Snetterton, GB	76.22
Mar. 21	Saloon over 1200cc	Ford Cortina Lotus	Oulton Park, GB	81.64
Mar. 21	Sports over 1200cc	Cooper Climax Monaco T49	Oulton Park, GB	90.90
Mar. 30	Formula 3	Cooper BMC T72	Goodwood, GB	92.47
Apr. 11	Formula 3	Cooper BMC T72	Oulton Park, GB	88.45
Apr. 18	Formula 3	Cooper BMC T72	Aintree, GB	84.63
May 2	Formula 3	Cooper BMC T72	Silverstone, GB	98.07
May 9	Formula 3/Heat	Cooper BMC T72	Monte Carlo, MC	65.08
May 9	Formula 3/Final	Cooper BMC T72	Monte Carlo, MC	65.97
May 17	Formula 3	Cooper BMC T72	Mallory Park, GB	83.80
May 17	GT up to 1600cc	Lotus Elan	Mallory Park, GB	84.85
June 13	GT over 1600cc	Jaguar E-type	Crystal Palace, GB	74.11
June 13	GT up to 1600cc	Lotus Elan	Crystal Palace, GB	74.61
June 13	Jaguar XKs	Jaguar XK 120	Crystal Palace, GB	71.88
June 28	Formula 3/Part 1	Cooper BMC T72	Rouen, F	—
June 28	Formula 3/Part 2	Cooper BMC T72	Rouen, F	—
	(Overall winner at average speed of 93.73 mph)			
July 5	Formula 3	Cooper BMC T72	Reims, F	108.10
Aug. 3	GT up to 2500cc	Lotus Elan	Brands Hatch, GB	82.81
Aug. 15	Marlboro 12 hrs., saloon cars	Ford Cortina Lotus	Marlboro, USA	53.55
Aug. 23	Formula 2/Heat	Lotus Cosworth 32	Zolder, B	92.29
Aug. 30	Formula 3	Cooper BMC T72	Zandvoort, NL	89.96
Sept. 19	Formula 3	Cooper BMC T74	Oulton Park, GB	90.91
Sept. 26	Formula 2	Lotus Cosworth 32	Snetterton, GB	97.94
Dec. 12	Rand GP, Formula 1/Heat	Lotus Climax 33	Kyalami, ZA	—

1965

				mph
May 5	Daily Express Trophy, Formula 1	BRM P261	Silverstone, GB	111.60
Sept. 12	Italian GP, Formula 1	BRM P261	Monza, I	130.46

1966

Jan. 22	Lady Wigram Trophy, Tasman	BRM P261	Christchurch, NZ	—
Jan. 29	Teretonga Trophy, Tasman	BRM P261	Invercargill, NZ	84.50
Feb. 27	Exide Cup, Tasman	BRM P261	Sandown Park, AUS	—
Mar. 5	Examiner 45, Tasman	BRM P261	Longford, AUS	—
Mar. 7	South Pacific C'ship, Tasman	BRM P261	Longford, AUS	115.96
May 22	Monaco GP, Formula 1	BRM P261	Monte Carlo, MC	76.50
Aug. 14	Formule Libre	Brabham Climax BT11	Surfers Paradise, AUS	—
Aug. 21	Rothmans 12-hrs, sports cars	Ferrari 250LM	Surfers Paradise, AUS	—
Oct. 9	Fuji 200, USAC Formula	Lola Ford T90	Mt. Fuji Spdwy., J.	103.46

1967

Jan. 7	New Zealand GP, Tasman	BRM P261	Pukekohe, NZ	100.90
Feb. 19	Australian GP, Tasman	BRM P261	Warwick Farm, AUS	87.67
Aug. 13	Formula 2	Matra Ford MS7	Karlskoga, S	—
Aug. 20	Formula 2	Matra Ford MS7	Enna, I	142.64
Sept. 16	Formula 2	Matra Ford MS7	Oulton Park, GB	106.18
Sept. 24	Formula 2	Matra Ford MS7	Albi, F	106.07

1968

Mar. 31	Formula 2	Matra Ford MS7	Montjuich Park, E	89.71
Apr. 21	Formula 2	Matra Ford MS7	Pau, F	74.93
June 23	Dutch GP, Formula 1	Matra Ford MS10	Zandvoort, NL	84.66
Aug. 4	German GP, Formula 1	Matra Ford MS10	Nürburgring, D	86.86
Aug. 17	Guards Gold Cup, Formula 1	Matra Ford MS10	Oulton Park, GB	109.29
Sept. 15	Formula 2	Matra Ford MS7	Reims, F	129.16
Oct. 6	United States GP, Formula 1	Matra Ford MS10	Watkins Glen, USA	124.89

1969

Mar. 1	South African GP, Formula 1	Matra Ford MS10	Kyalami, ZA	110.62
Mar. 16	Race of Champions Formula 1	Matra Ford MS80	Brands Hatch, GB	108.65
Apr. 7	Formula 2/Heat	Matra Ford MS7	Thruxton, GB	111.54
Apr. 27	Formula 2	Matra Ford MS7	Nürburgring, D	104.20
May 4	Spanish GP, Formula 1	Matra Ford MS80	Montjuich Park, E	93.89
May 11	Formula 2	Matra Ford MS7	Jarama, E	84.98
June 21	Dutch GP, Formula 1	Matra Ford MS80	Zandvoort, NL	111.04
July 6	French GP, Formula 1	Matra Ford MS80	Clermont-Ferrand, F	97.71
July 19	British GP, Formula 1	Matra Ford MS80	Silverstone, GB	127.25
Sept. 7	Italian GP, Formula 1	Matra Ford MS80	Monza, I	146.96